GW00630979

William Shakespeare: *As You Like It*

Collection CNED-Didier Concours
Capes / Agrégation d'Anglais

Daniel Defoe: Moll Flanders
Elisabeth Détis

George Herbert: The Temple
Marie Garnier-Giamarchi

Hanif Kureishi: The Buddha of Suburbia
Marc Porée

Katherine Mansfield: Selected Stories
Jean-Paul Pichardie

William Shakespeare: As You Like It
Pierre Iselin

N. Scott Momaday: House Made of Dawn
Bernadette Rigal-Cellard

Jean Toomer: Cane
Monica Michlin

Les Médias et l'information aux Etats-Unis depuis 1945
Daniel Royot et Susan Ruel, Nancy Kaplan, Pierre Mélandri, Sondra Rubenstein, Pierre Sicard

The Debate on a Republic for Australia
Jean-Claude Redonnet, Steve Garner

British Civilians in the Second World War (1939-1945)
Monica Charlot

Grammaire linguistique
Pierre Cotte

Manuel d'anglais oral pour les Concours + CD audio
Marc Fryd et Jean-Louis Duchet

© Didier Érudition - CNED, 1998
ISBN 2-86460-313-6

William Shakespeare:
As You Like It

Pierre ISELIN
François LAROQUE
Jean-Marie MAUGUIN

Didier Érudition
CNED, 1998

Table Of Contents

I. *As You Like It* in the Context of Shakespeare's Canon and of its Own Time

Shakespeare's career as a London dramatist spans, roughly speaking, the last decade of the sixteenth century and the first of the seventeenth century. We have a total of 38 plays (including *The Two Noble Kinsmen*).

If *As You Like It* was composed, as it is generally believed, in 1600, it comes at the half-way mark of Shakespeare's writing career and occupies the twentieth place or so in the list of the 38 plays that make up the canon.

The first decade of Shakespeare's composition (1590-1600) is usually perceived as the first phase of a set of three. It is dominated by the two most popular types of play at the time: comedies and history plays (especially plays inspired by English history). The second phase (1600-1607) includes the 'great' tragedies (*Hamlet, Othello, King Lear*, and *Macbeth*) and the so-called problem comedies, *i.e.*, comedies written in so black a vein as to lead spectator and critic to question the pertinence of the concept of comedy where *Troilus and Cressida, Measure for Measure*, and *All's Well That Ends Well* are concerned. The third and last phase (1608-1613) is almost uniquely comprised of those romances which are pastoral tragi-comedies (*Pericles, Cymbeline, The Winter's Tale, The Tempest, The Two Noble Kinsmen*). The one exception is *Henry VIII* returning as it does to the theme of English history of the most recent kind.

In his study of the development of Shakespearian comedy and romance, Northrop Frye isolates a group of comedies using the same basic structure:

> There is a group of comedies, including *The Two Gentlemen of Verona, As You Like It*, and *A Midsummer Night's Dream*, in which the action moves from a world of parental tyranny and irrational law into a forest.

There the comic resolution is attained, and the cast returns with it into their former world.[1]

In terms of dates of composition *The Two Gentlemen of Verona* is thought by Stanley Wells and Gary Taylor to be Shakespeare's first play and they assign it to 1590-91.[2] *A Midsummer Night's Dream* belongs to 1595 or thereabouts. Bringing up the rear, *As You Like It* makes use of the characteristic 'green-world' feature in 1600. The 'green-world' comedies thus occur with odd regularity in the first phase of Shakespeare's play-writing.

Other plays within and without this first period of composition show features that come close to the recognized pattern. Thus *The Merry Wives of Windsor* (1597-98) has Falstaff paid off for his attempted seduction and deception of the wives in an ordeal of singeing and pinching in the nocturnal wood where the whole community unites to perform the vengeful rite. Places other than a forest understood *stricto sensu* fulfil a similar purgative function: Portia's Belmont in *The Merchant of Venice* (1596-97) supplies the miraculous energies that can untie the tragic knot tightened among the trade and bustle of the large merchant city. In *The Tempest* (1611), two parties of royal misdoers from Naples and Milan are drawn by Prospero's magic to the island to repent and be cured before sailing home, better men than they were nearly all of them. The pastoral element of *As You Like It*, which I want to distinguish as clearly as possible from the forest element, is initially developed as an escapist utopian dream by Henry VI (Part III; 2.5.1-54).[3] The forest element plays some part too in this drama (3.1). The weak king is finally captured by game-keepers who are strolling in the woods where they intend to shoot harts. It is the royal hart whom they accidentally encounter and make prisoner. *The*

---

1.   *A Natural Perspective* (New York, London: 1965), pp. 140-41.
2.   *William Shakespeare: A Textual Companion* (Oxford: 1987), p. 109.
3.   With the exception of *AYL*, for which I follow Alan Brissenden's edition for the World's Classics (Oxford: 1993), all references to Shakespeare's plays are to Stanley Wells' and Gary Taylor's edition of *The Complete Works* (Oxford, 1988). For the sake of clarity, I stick however to '*Henry VI, Part III*' where the two editors choose to revert to the original title: *Richard Duke of York*.

Winter's Tale (1609) is the play best known for its use of pastoral with the fully-developed sheep-shearing feast in Act 4. By then, the deadly bear proves by its very presence that the world of the forest is not far from the fields where shepherds graze their sheep (3.3). But, although fatal, the brute is no more than a trace of the woodland world and the dangers lurking there. In *Cymbeline* (1610), the conventional opposition between the wicked court and the regenerative country is strongly made as a rebel courtier abducts the two young sons of the king of Britain to foster them in the heart of wild Wales. They live in a cave as Duke Senior does or Prospero on his island.

As You Like It is often paired off with *Twelfth Night*, although the latter stands firmly beyond the pale of the green-world comedies. The reason for the association is that the two plays come last of the happy comedies just before Shakespeare's inspiration takes a sombre course. Both are distinctly romantic comedies, written by a dramatist in the full maturity of his talent. Both share an element of provocation in the title which is calculated to yield nothing of the author's intention: *As You Like It, Twelfth Night or What You Will*. I have assimilated elsewhere the desultoriness of these non-titles to the light-headedness known to affect climbers at high altitude.[4] Total availability of his powers appears to induce a slight narcosis in Shakespeare. This is stylistically more visible perhaps in *As You Like It* which inherits much of the sophistication, raciness, and passionate love of double-entendre displayed by *Love's Labour's Lost* (1594-95). The masque elements of the latter play anticipate on the masque of Hymen in *As You Like It*, although they are of a different nature, especially if Hymen's masque is played straightforwardly as a *deus ex machina* resolution rather than as a rustic entertainment. If we are actually intended to see the pagan god of marriage then we are facing a theophany closer in tone to those in *Pericles* (scene 21), *Cymbeline* (5.5), and *The Tempest* (4.1).[5] On

---

4.   *William Shakespeare* (Paris: 1996), pp. 447-63.
5.   The betrothal masque of *The Tempest* is not strictly speaking a theophany but an illusion induced by Prospero's magic art.

the other hand, Rosalind's dependence on a supposed proficiency in white magic (5.2.56-59) announces the Paulina of *The Winter's Tale* and her clever staging of Hermione's resurrection in the statue scene at the end of the play. Is it surprising, anyway, that a play written at the half-way mark of Shakespeare's career should reveal as many ties with plays that precede it as it does with plays that follow? The rivalry for power between two brothers—a strong archetypal feature of great founding myths, like that of Rome with the twins Remus and Romulus—is a case in point. It appears in *Richard III* (1592-93) and *Titus Andronicus* (1592). It is an issue in *Much Ado About Nothing* (1598). It is doubly illustrated in *As You Like It* and reappears as a major feature of *Hamlet* (1601) a year later or so.

There are more immediate contextual influences at work on *As You Like It*, if we accept 1600 as the most likely year for its birth. The Globe was built and opened on Bankside—the south bank of the Thames—the year before, in 1599. With its thatched roof it was distinctive among the London amphitheatres and stood then as the last word in terms of theatre-building craft. Shakespeare's company, The Chamberlain's Men, had made a bold, if forced move, when they abandoned The Theatre, well north of the City wall to establish themselves no more than fifty yards from Philip Henslowe's successful Rose theatre. This manifests a time-honoured commercial and sociological pattern: a successful establishment will draw others of the same type in its immediate environment. Built in 1576, the first playhouse in London, the Theatre, had seen a second theatre, called the Curtain, built close to its site the following year. There must have been a conscious effort on the part of Shakespeare and the whole company to produce outstanding plays to attract crowds to their brand new space. *Henry V*, *Julius Caesar* and *As You Like It* are the tokens of their efforts. Henry V alludes to 'this wooden O,' Jaques announces: 'All the world's a stage, / And all the men and women merely players' (2.7.139-40), a glossing of the Globe's motto, itself derived from a phrasing of Petronius: *Totus mundus agit histrionem.* Hamlet will refer to 'this distracted Globe.' In 1601, the new playhouse, unlike the proverbial nine day's wonder, is still the talk of the town and

Shakespeare's characters are carefully fuelling the attraction of its name.

Political or military events make their mark also. If one can gloss 'The howling of the Irish wolves against the moon' (5.2.110-11) as Alan Brissenden does in the World's Classics edition as a reference to Irish moonworship and lycanthropy, the phrase in Elizabethan ears probably rang as a closer echo of the stalemating of the earl of Essex—the close friend of the earl of Southampton, Shakespeare's patron and dedicatee of *Venus and Adonis* and *The Rape of Lucrece*—by the head of the Irish revolt, the Earl of Tyrone. Essex had bravely left London in March of 1599 promising to come back with the Irish rebellion broached on his sword. *Henry V* vibrates with this hope (Chorus to Act 5). However, the commander of the English expeditionary force was back in London at the end of September of the same year, to face Elizabeth's displeasure, having made an inglorious truce with the cunning and mighty Irish wolf.

The abundant satirical passages[6] of the play as well as the merciless lampooning of Jaques as self-elected satirist-jester by Duke Senior (2.7.62-69)[7] are inseparable from the burning, on the 4th of June 1599, in the Hall of the Company of Stationers by order of the Archbishop of Canterbury—in charge of the censorship of publications—of scandalous books that had slipped into print unimpeached by his and the Bishop of London's deputy censors. The books in question all inclined to satire of the bitter sort, often mixed with bawdry. They included popular works.[8] Other works were to be stayed such as *Caltha*

---

6.   The play contains a satire of knights and their all-important sense of honour (1.2.59-75), of French foppishness through Monsieur Le Beau, of the Italianate Englishman (4.1.30-34), of novelty (1.1.92-93 and 1.2.86ff), of dissemblers (1.3.120-21), of the degeneration of manners (2.3.59ff), of the licensed fool as satirist (2.7.35ff), of women through Rosalind's denigration of them in her exchanges with Orlando, of the transvestite woman satirizing her own kind (4.1.184-87), of the duelling code (5.4.64ff), of male spectators in the Epilogue.

7.   It is characteristic of Shakespeare's method to use satire and also turn it upon the satirist. This twoedgedness is not only an insurance against censorship but the result of what seems to have been a trait of his nature.

8.   John Marston's *The Metamorphosis of Pygmalions image and certaine satyres* (1598), *The Scourge of Villainy* (1598), Edward Guilpin's *Skielethia, or a shadow of truth* (1598), the Snarling Satires, Sir John Davies' Epigrams with Marlowe's Elegies (1590), etc.

Poetarum, Hall's *Satires*, and *Willobie his Avisa*,[9] where the author Henry Willoby, educated in St John's and Exeter College, Oxford, broaches the popular and politically risky theme of Queen Elizabeth's past marriage plans and possibly alludes to sentimental hardships suffered by William Shakespeare.[10] The books of Gabriel Harvey and Thomas Nashe were to be seized wherever found and future writing by them stopped from getting into print. The whole affair was the result of the political scandal aroused by the publication in 1599 of John Hayward's history of Henry IV,[11] containing an account of the deposition of Richard II and a dedication in which he extolled the deserts of the Earl of Essex, now out of favour with Queen Elizabeth and soon to rebel in 1601.[12] One of the consequences of the crisis was to suddenly stave off the flow of thitherto popular English history plays. Shakespeare, like the other dramatists, deserted the vein which he had so far brilliantly illustrated. In the comedy of *As You Like It* Shakespeare finds, under the mask of a more universal and therefore less dangerous genre and on the basis of an unprinted text, an occasion to take up the satirical spear so recently torn from the hands of other writers in print. It is possible, however, that the vexed question of the 'staying entries' connected with the registration *As You Like It*, *Henry V*, *Everyman in his Humour*, and *Much Ado About Nothing* by the printer James Roberts may be in one way or another[13] connected with the awakened suspicion of the authorities after the reported conflicts.

Other less massive reflections of the historical and social or artistic context are to be found. Touchstone is very possibly the first Fool's role written for the company's new clown, Robert Armin, who had recently joined the Chamberlain's Men after

---

9. Registered and published in 1594.
10. See B. N. De Luna, *The Queen Declined: An Interpretation of "Willobie His Avisa"* (Oxford: 1970), J.-M. et A. Maguin, *William Shakespeare* (Paris: 1996), p. 358ff.
11. *The first part of the life and raigne of King Henrie IIII* (1599).
12. Hayward's dedication was to be used as evidence of treachery at the earl's trial.
13. Either on explicit order from the censors or through caution on the part of the printer.

his predecessor William Kempe, one of the original shareholders of the Globe in February 1599, had sold his share and left the company to go and dance the morris from London all the way to Norwich. Robert Armin is supposed to have had a more delicate style of acting than Kempe, as best suggested by the part of the Fool in *King Lear*. He started in life as apprentice to a goldsmith which might have prompted Shakespeare to call the Fool in *As You Like It,* Touchstone. The sexual allusion to 'stone' meaning 'testicle' is simultaneously possible, while John Stone, a tavern fool, who had acquired a certain renown in the inns of London offers another possible key.

On the musical front, it is not merely incidental, though, that the song in 5.3.14ff 'It was a lover and his lass' should turn up with slightly different words in Thomas Morley's *First Book of Ayres or Little Short Songes, to Sing and Play to the Lute*, published in 1600. *As You Like It* is Shakespeare's most musical play, and certainly the one whose structure most obviously serves the purpose of introducing song material as appears from 4.2 and 5.3.

The search for topical allusions is an important part of the critical and editorial game since these, if identified, may help date the play precisely. The asset though is not gilt-edged when we are confronted with a Folio-text-only play. Nearly a quarter of a century after composition, the text we are facing has had a lot of time to change and acquire new topical references and either shed or retain the old ones. This has encouraged some to see an allusion to the death of Marlowe in the phrase 'it strikes a man more dead than a great reckoning in a little room' (3.3.11-12). Marlowe had been killed on the 30th of May 1593 after allegedly quarrelling over the bill, or 'reckoning,' in a tavern at Deptford. However, the phrase contrasting the size of the bill with that of the premises where it is incurred is nearly proverbial and it is quite superfluous to recruit the help of a particular instance to justify its occurrence. To use this argument to push the play as far early as 1593, as some have done, is clearly ill-advised and certainly runs into major difficulties when it has to explain why such a popular play is not listed in 1598 among the rest of Shakespeare's works to-date by Francis Meres in *Palladis Tamia: Wit's Treasury*.[14] On the other hand, there is a clear allusion to Marlowe in 3.5.82-83 when Phoebe remarks: 'Dead shepherd, now I find thy saw of might: / Who ever loved that loved not at first sight?' Phoebe quotes a line from *Hero and Leander* written by Marlowe and finished by Chapman. The volume was published in 1598. The word 'shepherd' is possibly connected with one of Marlowe's poems 'The Passionate Shepherd to his Love' which opens with the famous line 'Come live with me, and be my love.'

Finally, *As You Like It* offers another more intemporal curiosity in being the play where a source narrative—Lodge's *Rosalynde* (1590)—offers the dramatist a banner printed with a name after his heart: Arden. The word means 'forest' just as 'Avon' in Stratford and elsewhere means 'river.' It is not only a topographical clue, but, as Peter Levi has shown,[15] a sociological one. The people who live in Stratford's Arden, the (ex)forest area opposed to 'Fielden' or fields, are prone to be conservative in economic, social, and religious terms. Corin's sheep are definitely not popular beasts in Shakespeare's Stratford where the pressure of local gentry like Edward Greville is for the increase of enclosures. In the eyes of the original grain- or hay-growing farmers, the sheep has turned into a ravening wolf devouring their substance.[16] The Shakespeares seem to have inclined to Arden in the local context. Shakespeare's father, John, did so when he married the daughter of his father's landlord, Mary Arden. Whichever way the argument is considered, it can no more be denied that every time 'Arden' occurs in the play's text, Shakespeare happens to have written his mother's name, in the same way that a year or so later the name 'Hamlet' is bound to refer him to his dead son's name.

---

14. This work is the most reliable chronological piece of evidence we have on plays written by Shakespeare prior to 1598.
15. *The Life and Times of William Shakespeare* (London: 1988).
16. The image is a popular motif encountered in various writings such as Philip Stubbes' *The Anatomy of Abuses* (1583), or in contemporary ballads.

One should be careful not to make too much or too little of such coincidences. To have brought in briefly (5.1), to be ridiculed by Touchstone, a William born in Arden can hardly be less than a teaser. Is it possible that the dramatist who is, rightly or wrongly, alleged to have taken the part of Adam in the play doubled as William of Arden, the rustic clown? Three 'bit-parts' in the play, more or less closely connected with Arden can certainly be seen to uphold traditional values: Adam, who follows his young master into the forest and shuns the world of hatred identified with Frederick's 'new' court and Oliver; Sir Oliver Martext, fairly reeking of ignorance as well as of the 'old' religion;[17] William, the forest-born, suitor of Audrey neatly dislodged, nay drummed from his suit, by his urban rival, Touchstone. Whether Shakespeare, in writing the play, saw himself as being in charge of interpreting all three parts, or two, or none, only the original William of Arden could tell. However, through we cannot be quite sure, it remains that the play world and the world of the dramatist's Warwickshire have strong features in common.

J.-M. MAGUIN

---

17. It is tempting to think he might have been modelled on John Frith, an old priest in Temple Grafton near Stratford, which some identify as the place where William Shakespeare married Anne Hathaway on grounds of discretion. Apart from catholic leanings, John Frith evinced a good measure of indifference towards ecclesiastical caution. He is known to have disregarded the publication of banns, necessary before the marriage ceremony. He is also known to have been close to nature and especially gifted at nursing hurt falcons back to health.

II. *As You Like It* and the Traditions of Comedy

Comedy as a genre is not easily analysed since it looks as volatile as protean. Furthermore, there is no general or theoretical model for it, contrary to tragedy which is strictly defined by Aristotle in his *Poetics*.

In order to identify and analyse the elements of comedy in *As You Like It*, the play has to be replaced within a larger tradition and in the perspective of Shakespearean comedy with its own specific growth from farce to tragicomic romance.

As You Like It stands at the crossroads between the early slapstick of *The Comedy of Errors* or *The Taming of the Shrew* and the moving wonders of the last plays. It is pastoral or satirical only in appearance as it seems more concerned with examining the intellectual issues of liberty and theatricality (disguise, gender, role-playing, etc.) or with the discussion of the follies of love or misanthropy.

As such, it is quite different from the rest of Shakespeare's comedies and looks ahead to the great tragedies like *Hamlet* or *King Lear*.

Contrary to tragedy, in Aristotle's analysis, where tragic catharsis or purgation is defined as a combination of pity and terror, there is no theoretical model for comedy. Etymology traces the word back to the Greek word *komos*, meaning procession or orgy, which would seem to connect the genre with ancient fertility rites associated with Dionysos. In the Induction of *The Taming of the Shrew*, Christopher Sly mistakes the word for 'comonty,' thus revealing the links between comedy and the community at large or with the common people, as opposed to tragedy which usually involves kings and princes and the affairs of state.

There are basically two main types of comic strategy. The first uses laughter to mock at some deficiency or error or vice in a character who is revealed to be foolish or odious. Its traditional motto is thus 'Castigat ridendo mores' (it punishes manners by laughter). This is corrective comedy. The second type ties comedy up with rejoicing and carnival by sparking off a form of convivial laughter where mirth and foolery are in order. This is what C. L. Barber called 'festive comedy.'

These two types of derisive and festive laughter may be equated with laughter and delight as Sir Philip Sidney defined them in *An Apology for Poetrie* (1595):

> Delight hath a joy in it, either permanent or present. Laughter hath only a scornful tickling . . . We are ravished with delight to see a fair woman . . . We laugh at deformed creatures . . . wherein we cannot delight. We delight in good chances, we laugh at mischances . . .

Mirth reveals an exuberance and a gaiety or geniality that made it a curative or therapeutic instrument (Rabelais, a physician by trade, claimed that he had written his books to make his patients laugh and thus cure them). Nicholas Udall, the author of the first English comedy, *Ralph Roister Doister* (ca 1550), endorses this view:

> For mirth prolongeth life, and causeth health
> Mirth recreated our spirits and voideth pensiveness . . .

Mirth is presented as a cure for melancholy, as a means to dispell the darker humours of the body (spleen or black bile) and thus as an effective and efficient agent of good health. Another illustration of this is found in the Induction of *The Taming of the Shrew*; a Messenger says to the drunken Sly, whom he addresses as if he were a great Lord, as he wakes up from his intoxicated slumber:

> Your honour's players, hearing your amendment,
> Are come to play a pleasant comedy;
> For so your doctors hold it very meet,
> Seeing too much sadness hath congeal'd your blood,
> And melancholy is the source of frenzy.
> Therefore they thought it good you hear a play
> And frame your mind to mirth and merriment,
> Which bars a thousand harms and lengthens life. (Induction, 129-36)

In *As You Like It*, Rosalind's 'holiday humour' (4.1.62-63) and contagious gaiety when disguised as Ganymede is an antinomy, if not an antidote, to Jaques's 'sullen fits' (2.1.67) and it goes alongside with the jolly songs of the foresters. Now, the main disease or madness which Rosalind-Ganymede means to cure is love (3.2.381-85), as in the *Treatise on Lovesickness* by the French physician Jacques Ferrand. But the 'love cure' in the play is just one of the games or sports devised by Rosalind in the forest and, according to the pattern of most Shakespearean comedies, the true cure for love turns out to be marriage, when 'delights' are made to rhyme with rites in the play's concluding couplet!

If we now consider the history of the genre, the main categories of classical times were Old and New comedy. Old comedy goes back to Aristophanes (448 ?-380 BC), *i.e.* to bawdy and satirical plays with little individual characterization and where caricature and buffoonery prevail (as in *The Frogs*, *The Clouds* or *Lysistrata* . . .)

New comedy was represented by Terence and Plautus in Rome. Its main pattern is what Northrop Frye describes as a 'comic Oedipus situation' since it presents the successful efforts of a young man to outwit a rival suitor in order to woo and win the girl of his heart's choice. The rival or opponent is usually the young man's father (*senex*) and the chosen girl is often a slave or courtesan whom the denouement reveals in fact to be of high birth (*cognitio*) and thus marriageable. In New comedy, the young triumph in the end and they overrule the opposition of the *senex iratus*. Parental will usually has the force of law in the comedies (see Egeus calling upon the 'old Law' of Athens in *A Midsummer Night's Dream* to oppose the choice of Lysander by his daughter Hermia) and the *senex* is often jealous or the slave of some sort of mental bondage (see Celia's 'My father's rough and envious disposition,' 1.2.225). The plot of comedy serves as a rite of passage for the young.

This is taken up by the Canadian critic Northrop Frye in his well-known article, 'The Argument of Comedy' (1949), to illustrate his thesis of a ritual background to comedy. Frye speaks of the ritual of the struggle, death and resurrection of a god-man linked to the cycle of the seasons in which spring yearly triumphs over winter, which offers a parallel for comedy:

We may call this the drama of the green world, and its theme is once again the triumph of life over the waste land, the death and revival of the year impersonated by figures still human, and once divine as well . . .

Comedy is thus seen as post-tragic (tragedy is indeed only a prelude to comedy as we see in Dante's *La Divina commedia* which takes us from 'Inferno' to 'Paradiso'). Wylie Sypher presents a similar interpretation in a book on comedy:

> Comedy . . . is essentially a carrying away of Death, a triumph over mortality by some absurd faith in rebirth, restoration, salvation . . .

In *As You Like It*, Orlando's extraordinary triumph against the 'sinewy Charles,' Duke Frederick's wrestler (and killer), like his bare-handed combat against the hungry lioness makes him a figure of survival, even of revival. His wounded arm amounts to a form of symbolic death. The sending of the 'bloody napkin' to Ganymede, which brings about his/her fainting is reminiscent of the story of 'Pyramus and Thisbe' (adapted from Ovid's *Metamorphoses*), the prototype for Romeo and Juliet's *Liebestod*, or cult of deadly love. Orlando is thus indirectly assimilated to a vegetation 'god,' to Adonis slain by the boar to the great despair and frustration of Venus, a story which Shakespeare dealt with in his narrative poem *Venus and Adonis*. But, contrary to Adonis, metamorphosed into a flower, Orlando recovers, just as Ganymede's fainting, or 'mock death,' is called 'counterfeiting.'

This brings about the wonders of Celia's and Oliver's meeting and love at first sight, a miraculous transformation (''Twas I, but 'tis not I,' 4.3.136) foreshadowing Frederick's conversion at the end. All of a sudden, the 'obstacles' are removed as the blocking figures are touched by the 'magic' of the green world. According to Frye, this follows

> the earlier traditions established by Peele and developed by Lyly, Greene and the masque writers, which use themes from romance and folklore . . . These themes are largely medieval in origin and derive . . . from . . . the drama of folk ritual . . . and . . . the dramatic activity that punctuated the Christian calendar with the rituals of an immemorial paganism. We may call this the drama of the green world.

In *The Sceptre of Saturn. Shakespeare and Magical Thinking* (1994), Linda Woodbridge calls this 'countryside comedy . . . which remained the most magical of genres, partly because it owed much to pastoral, whose links to fertility magic are clear . . . ' (pp. 185-86). 'The action of comedy,' says Frye, 'begins in a world represented as a normal world, moves into the green world, goes into a metamorphosis there in which the comic resolution is achieved, and returns to a normal world.' This does not exactly correspond to *As You Like It*, since the newcomers in the forest (Oliver and Duke Frederick) mean to stay there after their 'conversion,' while Jaques also decides to change courts and Dukes to learn 'out of these convertites' and to 'stay at your abandoned cave' (5.4.179, 191).

For Northrop Frye, the *telos*, or end, of greenworld comedy is sexual consummation (' . . . in these degrees have they made a pair of stairs to marriage, which they will climb incontinent, or else be incontinent before marriage' (5.2.35-36). Touchstone also jocularly refers to the 'country copulatives' (5.4.54-55). But in *The Shakespearian Wild* (1991), Jeanne Addison Roberts makes the point that the true argument of comedy is not consummation but delay:

> Shakespeare shows impressive variety and skill in designing strategies of pleasure enhancing delay . . .

This is the particular game played by Rosalind as Ganymede, who pretends to perform a love cure on the man she loves and who engages in a mock marriage which she wishes were a real ceremony. 'Much virtue in if,' as Touchstone says at the end of his speech on the Seven Causes of Quarrel (5.4.98)!

Quite different from greenwood or countrylife comedy which was coming to an end in 1599, the new fashionable genre had become city comedy under the influence of Ben Jonson:

> Our Scene is London, 'cause we would make knowne,
> No countries mirth is better than our owne.
> No clime breeds better matter, for your whore,
> Bawd, squire, imposter, many persons more,
> Whose manners, now called humours, feed the stage:
> And which have still been subject, for the rage
> Or spleene of comick writers . . . (*The Alchemist* [1610], Prologue 5-11)

This English version of New comedy is a comedy of manners or of 'humours' satirizing contemporary vices and follies in the great Metropolis, London, by presenting a gallery of grotesque types made of swindlers and gulls. Jonson founded his comic theory and structure on the medicinal theory of the four humours—blood, phlegm, choler, or yellow bile, melancholy, or black bile, whose 'temperament' or mixture was supposed to determine a man's condition and character. A lack of balance in one humour produced four types of disposition—sanguine, phlegmatic, choleric and melancholic. Jonson explains these comic principles in the famous prologue of *Every Man Out of His Humour* (1599), a play performed at the Globe by the Chamberlain's Men, Shakespeare's company:

> ASPER   ... in every human body,
> The choler melancholy, phlegm and blood,
> By reason that they flow continually
> In some one part, and are not continent,
> Receive the name of humours. Now thus far
> It may, by metaphor, apply itself
> Unto the general disposition:
> As when some one peculiar quality
> Doth so possess a man, that it doth draw
> All his effects, his spirits, and his powers,
> In his confluctions, all run one way.
> This may be truly said to be a humour ...
> CORDATUS   ... Now if an idiot
> Have but an apish or fantastic strain,
> It is his humour.
> ASPER   Well, I will scourge those apes,
> And to the courteous eyes oppose a mirror
> As large as the stage whereon we act,
> Where they shall see the time's deformity
> Anatomised in every nerve, and sinew
> With constant courage and contempt of fear ...
> (*Every Man Out of His Humour* [1599] Prologue 5-21)

Most of Jonson's comic figures fall into two complementary types, the victim or gull on the one hand, and, on the other, the trickster or con-man who fleeces and mocks him. It is a world of eccentricity and excess often verging on the grotesque. In the end, there usually occurs a reversal of situations which finally tricks and exposes the main trickster, so that a corrective sense of morality is achieved.

In *As You Like It*, Duke Frederick ('the Duke is humorous,' 1.2.251), Jaques ('most humorous sadness,' 4.1.18-19), Touchstone ('a poor humour of mine own sir,' 5.4.57-58) or Rosalind ('I am in a holiday humour,' 4.1.63) may certainly all be regarded as humour characters. Rosalind, who masquerades as Ganymede during most of the play, plays the part of the trickster, pulling the strings and manipulating situations and characters all along acts 2 to 5. But, if she is exposed in the end as the 'woman' she is beneath her masculine attire, it is only to work towards general reconciliation and harmony and in order to make the final quadruple wedding possible. She is a benevolent trickster, moved or inspired by a theology of love and goodness rather than selfish evil as in Jonson. *As You Like It* thus contains the seeds of the 'comedy of humours' which will be allowed to show through Shakespeare's next and last romantic comedy, *Twelfth Night*, and fully bloom in his 'problem comedies,' *All's Well That Ends Well* and *Measure for Measure*, far more bitter and biting in tone and content.

In *As You Like It*, Shakespeare exploits the new model of the 'comedy of humours' but he counterbalances extremes or opposites in the incessant confrontations which he organizes between his characters as Rosalind vs Touchstone, Touchstone vs Jaques, Jaques *vs* Rosalind, etc. Jaques's melancholy is matched by Rosalind's sanguine 'holiday humour' as saturnine fits are subverted by the growing saturnalian mood that prevails at the end. In the meantime, a form of clarification is obtained, thus taking the spectator of the play from 'release' to 'clarification,' a movement which, according to C. L. Barber, corresponds to the main patterns of festive comedy. We thus find confrontation and combination of two antagonist types of comedy—festive or greenworld comedy and the comedy of humours in which Jaques's speech on the Seven Ages of man is a masterpiece of the genre. But if the satiric is integrated within the general scheme of *As You Like It*, it is downplayed and benign as satire is itself being satirized in the character of Jaques, Arden's all too predictable malcontent.

As Harold Jenkins has remarked, *As You Like It* is 'conspicuously lacking in comedy's more robust and boisterous elements—the pomps of Dogberry [the malapropist head of the city watch in *Much Ado About Nothing*] and the romps of sir Toby [Olivia's bibulous uncle in *Twelfth Night*].' In the *Henry IV* plays, the trickster is Sir John Falstaff, a colourful carnival figure whose appetite and enormous bulk release considerable comic energy while he himself is made the butt of Prince Hal's jokes, acerbic comments or insults. This is the punching ball principle which is repeated at the level of farce in another Falstaff play, *The Merry Wives of Windsor*, where the fat knight is baited, trapped and humiliated as a punishment for his lust when he is disguised as Herne the Hunter in act 5. In *As You Like It*, Rosalind-Ganymede, though witty enough, is all too lean and she fails to deploy real carnivalesque buoyancy or stategy, even though she is in drag. Touchstone, in spite of his many bawdy jokes, would come closer to a carnivalesque figure as he is someone who is constantly aware of his bodily needs whether it means giving a rest to his weary legs or satisfying his sexual desires (see, in that respect, his cynical courting of Audrey, the goat girl).

The problem is that the 'good life' in Arden is found 'in the riches of deprivation rather than in the poverty of prodigality' as Ruth Nevo puts it. Duke Senior does not favour a comic economy which would require expense or excess. He plays the part of a Stoic philosopher, taking a Spartan stance that allows him to enjoy the 'sweet' 'uses of adversity' (2.1.12) and to behave as a patient but happy moralist. Rosalind embodies comic pleasure and the liberation of playful fantasies but that is mostly confined to the level of language, conversation and a series of ambiguous games played with Orlando. As Ruth Nevo finally puts it, 'in a comedy supposed to triumph over death by some "absurd faith" [Wylie Sypher], Touchstone may epitomize the absurdity and Rosalind the faith.' This indeed is a paradoxical partnership, an incongruous pairing of opposites that would seem to characterize Shakespeare's 'post-Falstaffian comedies' (Nevo), namely *Much Ado About Nothing*, *As You Like It*, and *Twelfth Night*.

In fact, Shakespearean comedy is supposed to promote a form of self-knowledge through a deflation of illusions and an adjustment of its characters to reality. Orlando begins with 'mutiny' (1.1.21), instinctively rejecting the fraternal bondage which keeps him uneducated like a 'peasant.' He wants to become a gentleman according to his nature and his blood and he aims at the construction of his identity rather than at reaching self-knowledge as such. His passage into the world of the forest will provide him with an occasion for his 'self-fashioning' (S. Greenblatt). But, paradoxically, the education he will receive will be the love lessons of Rosalind-Ganymede, so that, for him, the woods become a 'school for love.'

Rosalind-Ganymede cruelly and brutally pricks the bubble of Phoebe's pretensions by holding a mirror up to her real 'value':

> [To Silvius]   'Tis not her glass but you that flatters her . . .
> [To Phoebe]   But mistress, know yourself . . .
> Sell when you can, you are not for all markets. (3.5.55-61)

Her function is to rebuke or debunk most characters in Arden's fantastic gallery (See Jaques in 4.1.30-34, or Silvius in 4.3.68-71). Orlando calls Jaques a fool in inviting him to look at the fool in the river (3.2.276-80). But the intrigues of the forest are also a revelation for Rosalind herself, as she exclaims:

> Alas, poor shepherd, searching of thy wound
> I have by hard adventure found my own. (2.4.41-42)

The fool in Arden is used to anatomize the 'wise man's folly' (Jaques in 2.7.56). Satire and medicine are metaphors for the expression of the truth which is obliquely or directly administered to most of the characters. Those who escape this are the convertees (Oliver, Duke Senior, and, up to a certain point, Jaques himself), who suddenly swing from one humorous excess to another, from evil to good, without taking the time to be confronted to reality.

Disguise and metamorphosis are both placed under the aegis of change and mutability in *As You Like It*. Sex-change and shape-shifting (mainly achieved stylistically through the numerous animal images in the play) are constantly referred to in this comedy. One of its emblematic images is the Wheel of Fortune (see Brutus 'There is a tide in the affairs of men,' *Julius*

Caesar, 4.2.272) with its incessant twists and turns, reversals and revolutions. As Thomas McFarlane writes in *Shakespeare's Pastoral Comedy* (1972):

> . . . comedy not only accepts artificiality but revels in it . . . Comedy not only employs disguise; it frolics in its permutations . . . The playful grotesquerie of the disguises are, in the artifice of the comic situation, accepted as proof against penetration.

As Ganymede (see 1.3.110-27 and 3.2.189-91), Rosalind turns herself into an epitome of change, caprice, whimsicality. This is revealed in the recurrence of the words 'giddy' and 'giddiness' in the play, as in 4.1.136-42:

> ROSALIND [to Orlando]   I will be more jealous of thee than a Barbary cock-pigeon over his hen, more clamorous than a parrot against rain, more new-fangled than an ape, more giddy in my desires than a monkey. I will weep for nothing, like Diana in the fountain, and I will do that when you are disposed to be merry. I will laugh like a hyena . . .

This gives an illustration of calculating femininity and of the traditional clichés about feminine contrariness and changeability, part and parcel of the stock-in-trade of anti-feminist satire or farce. On the other hand, Orlando is taken aback by the lightning speed at which Celia and Oliver fall in love:

> ORLANDO   Is't possible that on so little acquaintance you should like her? That but seeing, you should love her? and loving, woo? And wooing, she should grant? . . .
> OLIVER   Neither call the giddiness of it in question. (5.2.1-5)

The question of disguise is everywhere in this comedy. The phrase 'doublet and hose,' with its own linguistic marker of ambiguity (*doublet*) that connotes doubleness or even duplicity, is repeatedly used to refer to Rosalind's disguise in her masculine attire. At the same time, the disguise is only skin-deep and it does not affect what happens inside her, as Rosalind essentially remains a 'woman' behind her disguise:

> [To Celia]   Dost thou think, though I am caparisoned like a man I have a doublet and hose in my disposition? (3.2.188-90)

But the dividing line between disguise and disposition seems quite thin and problematic. Indeed, neither Orlando nor her own father manage to see through the surface Ganymede! This is of course part of the conventions and artifice of comedy, but it would seem that, in *As You Like It*, 'Cucullus facit monachum' (the cowl does make the monk)! Rosalind inventories the 'marks' of love (3.2.356-66) while Jaques's 'Seven ages of man' speech presents the stages of man's life in the form of a succession of stereotyped emblems or vignettes, with clockwork predictability as in the automata of Strasburg's cathedral. These are nothing but a series of roles (the image of the 'slippered Pantaloon' explicitly referring to *commedia dell'arte*) taken straight from the property basket. In the end, Rosalind asks the lovers to 'put on [their] best array' (5.2.68-69) while her own sartorial change will work wonders and will be regarded as the equivalent of magical transformation, that of the world of the theatre. Yet, she keeps a constant ambiguity in her successive parts. She is and she is not the man. She resorts to 'if,' to faining, feigning and fainting. Hers is the art of the counterfeit. As Greenblatt puts it:

> There are simple pleasures in life, but the theater is not one of them. To be sure, at its core, there seems to be a set of familiar, virtually timeless games, variations on the childhood theme of 'let's pretend.'

Metamorphosis, or change of form, is used in reference to Ovid, to Pythagoras' theory of metempsychosis, and it seems to work both ways. Men are assimilated to animals while beasts are anthropomorphized. Arden is both a fabulous word and a world of fable. Jaques ironically compares the four couples about to be wedded to the animals in Noah's ark (5.4.35-36). Touchstone is the one who constantly translates the human into the animal world (see for example 3.2.76-79). The hunters' 'horn song' in 4.2 erases the borderline between man and the natural world as the hunters wear the animals' 'leather skin and horns' (4.2.11). A similar assimilation occurs in another early Globe play, *Julius Caesar*, when Antony discovers that Caesar has just been stabbed to death:

> O world, thou wast the forest to this hart;
> And this indeed, a world, the heart of thee. (3.1.208-209)

Beyond the themes and ideas of disguise and metamorphosis, one finds the important notion of 'conversion' in *As You Like It*. It is the most spectacular expression of the healing powers, of the magic of the forest. Contrary to disguise, which is merely exterior, this is a deep inner tranformation.

This is a surprising element for *As You Like It* is often rightly presented as a discussion play where little actually occurs and where language and conversation bring about entertainment or education. The play provides a succession of dialogues, of verbal exchanges with statements and counter-statements instead of a given plot line (contrary to Shakespeare's other comedies, there is no sub-plot other than the to and fro movements from court to forest and back).

Touchstone is the life and soul of wit in the forest and his speeches are regularly studded with absurd and obscene innuendoes (see 2.4.10ff). When he refers to 'the wooing of a peascod instead of her [Jane Smile],' this is a malapropism which turns out to be a spoonerism or antistrophe to mean 'codpiece,' a most prominent piece of Renaissance male attire! At the same time, this serves as a sly adumbration of Orlando's wooing of Ganymede in the place of his Rosalind. Touchstone chortles at Corin's down to earth philosophy as he later debunks Orlando's romantic love by improvising a thirteen-line poem which is a scurrilous parody of the Petrarchan model:

> Such a nut is Rosalind.
> He that sweetest rose will find
> Must find love's prick, and Rosalind. (3.2.106-108)

Similarly, his pointed piece in prose on the Seven causes of quarrel is a *reductio ad absurdum* of Jaques' earlier recitation on the Seven ages of man. The fool is not only a master of nonsense, he is also a kind of archer, who, as Duke Senior says in the end, 'uses his folly like a stalking-horse, and under the presentation of that, he shoots his wit' (5.4.101-102). Earlier on (5.4.62), Touchstone had referred to 'the fool's bolt,' which establishes a connection between the shafts of Jaques' satire, which 'pierceth through the body of country, city, court' as the

First Lord said in 2.1.57-58 and the anatomy of absurdity practised in the kingdoms of folly.

Rosalind is another witty character in *As You Like It*. If Touchstone is indeed the 'whetstone of the wits' (1.2.51), she tends to imitate his favorite pieces with its alliterative jingles. The theme of wit is even the subject matter of a conversation between Orlando and Rosalind-Ganymede in 4.1.147-59. Such variations on 'woman's wit' are also double-entendres since the word 'wit' was also currently used in the sense of genitalia or sexual organs of both sexes. Woman's wit was then reputed to be as unstoppable as her tongue, a misogynist idea at the root of the constant parallels between language and sexuality. Desire is polymorphous and essentially conveyed through the channels of garrulous conversation and the ambiguous echoes of words as in Rosalind's exclamation: 'My affection hath an unknown bottom, like the bay of Portugal' (4.1.190-91), where there is a double play on the polysemy of 'bottom' and 'bay' (see '. . . the bay where all men ride' in Sonnet 137). Rosalind's 'holiday humour' finds its highest expression in counterfeiting and in playing games with Orlando as an invisible woman safely hidden behind her 'doublet and hose.' This may be regarded as an equivalent of masking in a carnival. Make-believe, pretending and wit serve Rosalind to come to terms with reality and to fulfil her deepest desires. She is a trickster heroine who has everything and almost everyone under control. Like Duke Senior, she finds 'good in everything' (2.1.17). Hers is a positive energy as she embodies the curative, stimulating powers of pastoral 'liberty' and discipline.

As You Like It follows neither the exact pattern of the other greenworld comedies marked by ritual and Saturnalian excess nor the corrective model of the Jonsonian comedy of humours or city comedy. This 'discussion play' is characterized by what Mikhaïl Bakhtin has called 'dialogism,' which consists in promoting a multiplicity of angle and viewpoints by using dialogue to put forward a relative or uncertain vision of life. There is no place, in such a world, for transcendental truth or for a superior, all-embracing point of view. Everything is scattered and multiple.

In the end, the blatant artifice of Hymen, the *deus ex machina* of comedy, is used to reinforce the self-conscious theatricality of a comedy that exposes its own artifice in order to offer a side-glance at the arbitrariness of the dramatic conventions and mechanisms on which it depends. *As You Like It* is a meta-comedy resorting to the usual devices in order to produce laughter and mirth but it also insists on distance and on tinges of playful irony. Rosalind's uncertain gender reflects the mixed genres of the play, while Touchstone calls attention to the 'motley' nature of its stylistic fabric or texture (*collage* or *bricolage*).

As You Like It can be seen as Shakespeare's *Praise of Folly*. It amounts to a cool examination of the traditions of comedy, all presented in an arbitrary, self-referential manner. As Anne Barton writes in her article 'Shakespeare's Sense of an Ending,' Shakespeare's 'classical comedy' is a 'unique combination of realism and romance.'

François LAROQUE

III. 'Motley's the only wear':
As You Like It, or the 'Bigarrure'

The green world of the Forest of Arden is also a world turned upside down. This reversibility of court and garden was in evidence in the stage setting created by Adrian Noble for the Royal Shakespeare Company in Stratford in 1985, in which the green of the pastoral scene corresponded tone for tone and object for object to the black of the court.[1]

Over this strange universe, which links the artificial and enchanted world of the pastoral with the facetious wit and rural English folklore of the Mummers and the Skimmington ride reigns the motley, the mottled livery of the court jester, but also a principle of assembly in which the arbitrary vies with the burlesque in matters of language as well as within the structure of the whole. The principle of 'bigarrure,' by which Etienne Tabourot, also known as des Accords, or Thoinot Arbeau, designates the ludic combinations of sounds and letters found in the riddles, the spoonerisms or antistrophes, the ambiguities, the backward verses and other word-play,[2] corresponds to the image given by this comedy. Its Surface unity—in reality just one *trompe l'œil* among many— barely mashs a play without plot or real action, one put together from bits and pieces, from confrontations between differing points of view, from reported conversations, from overlappings and dislocations.

For here all is a wink of the eye, a montage and mosaic of quotations. The forest is a poetic forum because the leaves and the bark of its trees serve for writing love poems. The violence which petrifies the world of the court seems miraculously to disperse and dissolve at the whim of the modulations and scales of the speeches and songs. If the court crystallizes the stakes of

---

1. "The world of the forest is but the green double of the black world of the court." Jean-Marie Maguin, *Cahiers Elisabéthains*, n° 28 (October 1985), p. 99.
2. Estienne Tabourot, *Les Bigarrures du Seigneur des Accords* (1588), ed. Francis Goyet, 2 vol., Droz, Genève 1986.

power, of possessing, the forest is the place of **being**, where word games are rolled out. Curiously, the only one who is left out of the *catharsis* of the discourse in its oral dimension is Orlando, who carries on in the forest his struggle for dignity, rights, and recognition. A new type of Hercules, David or Robin Hood, he 'somatizes' his dilemma with the help of gesture and action, or transcribes things through the medium of a mannered literary style. The forest will be the place of his education, a school of word and desire. Thus everything here seems to be played out between two poles, the didactic of desire on the one hand, and the motley of styles on the other.

The reason for this is that, unlike the other comedies of Shakespeare, in which the plot unfolds in several successive stages, criss-crossing the actions of mechanicals or of servants with that of lovers, merchants or princes, *As You Like It* does not assume this traditional division into primary and secondary plots. The one principle which prevails in Arden is that of the encounter; the characters follow each other onto the stage to expose their difficulties or their passions. By refusing to establish a hierarchy of the debates within closed worlds whose minor plots reflect, intersect or become entangled in the main plot, Shakespeare appears to be taking a positive step in the direction of Ben Jonson's comedy of humours. Indeed the central figure of Rosalind is a bit like 'Everywoman in her humour'!

The architecture and colouring of the dramatic text reflect this apparent 'laissez-faire, laissez-passer' approach. If free circulation and open exchanges characterize a comedy that uses the conventions of the pastoral to authorize the most audacious social juxtapositions, an apparent free and easy style marks the scenes in which dialogue in prose and verse follow each other (which, it is true, is hardly new in Shakespeare), along with poems of every sort, songs, and what can only be called 'recitations,' that is, various purple patches delivered in turn by the Old Duke, by Jaques, by Rosalind, Touchstone, etc. This amounts to saying that, if the style is marked by virtuosity, by pirouettes and verbal pyrotechnics, it is singularly lacking in consistency and unity. What is operating here is a generalized principle of transformation which assigns an essential role to invention, idiosyncrasy and unbridled fantasy. From then on, the attention of the reader or spectator is necessarily drawn to the artifice of the proceedings, which calls attention to itself as a choice of eclecticism, florilegium, or anthology.

In fact, the tirades and dialogues are sprinkled with allusions to the Bible, to Ovid's *Metamorphoses*, to the works of Christopher Marlowe, Spenser and numerous predecessors whom it would be tedious to enumerate. In a word, Shakespeare offers us pell-mell a pastoralizing, musical, satirical, heroic, burlesque or erotic selection, taking care to leave traces of the original label or seams of the fabric, to return to the image of the jester's livery. *As You Like It* is, for me, the comedy of *morceaux choisis*.

Indeed, everything is placed under the ensign of discourse. The exiled Duke has decided to make the best of a bad job and to be converted to the joys of simplicity, conviviality and pastoral hospitality, by adopting a style of life (2.1.20) that proceeds from a double activity of translation: translation from one place to another through exile, and a translation of the heart, an effort to turn misfortune into blessing, to 'translate the stubbornness of fortune into so quiet and so sweet a style' (2.1.19). By the double play of adaptation and alliteration, the forest becomes a temple with sermons in its stones, books in its brooks, and where trees have tongues (2.1.16-17). The hostile world of the wintry forest turns into a place of meditation, becoming an enchanted garden through the sole magic of a word that stirs up or accompanies a movement of spiritual conversion. No doubt one could find the equivalent of such an attitude, which is also a pose, in certain contemporary Chinese or Japanese texts. Inner serenity, a stone garden, a place in nature where one senses the breath of the spirit, and where animals appear as close kin to men, all of this evoking a vaguely Buddhist or zen acclimatation, but with roots also plunged into ancient philosophy (Stoicism, Pythagoreanism).

But, alongside this apparent unity-of-being rediscovered through contact with nature, *As You Like It* brings to the stage the comedy of fragmentation, of dissection and anatomical dispersion. This is one of the founding principles of the grotesque, to which I will return, *i.e.* to give privileged status, one by one, to different parts of the body, by equipping each with an autonomous language. The head, the mouth, the belly or the bottom thus become complete beings, characters in themselves. If Rosalind is the head, Orlando the legs, Touchstone the stomach and the private parts, Jaques the organ of what Rabelais called the 'matière joyeuse,' we see opposed to these a haughty Phoebe, a down-to-earth Audrey, in such a way that the image of the decomposed, then restored, body is lightly drawn like a kind of watermark, as an expression of the movement of dislocation and return which defines the general rhythm of the play.

Does not Jaques say of his predominant humour: '. . . it is a melancholy of mine own, compounded of *many simples*, extracted of *many objects*, and indeed the *sundry* contemplation of my travels . . .' (4.1.15-17)? All by himself, he is the one and the many, a case study for a future 'Anatomy of Melancholy,' a *Wunderkammer* or a walking curiosity chest. But the erotic eye is also the one which details and decomposes the parts of the loved body. Thus Phoebe declares to Silvius after Ganymede's departure:

> He is not very tall; yet for his years he's tall.
> His leg is but so-so; and yet 'tis well.
> There was a pretty redness in his lip,
> A little riper and more lusty red
> Than that mixed in his cheek. 'Twas just the difference
> Betwixt the constant red and mingled damask.
> There be some women, Silvius, had they marked him
> *In parcels* as I did, would have gone near
> To fall in love with him . . . (4.1.120-27)

This fragmentation of the erotic or eroticised body, of leg or cheek, is characteristic of the games of poetic heraldry that Shakespeare practiced freely elsewhere (in *Romeo and Juliet* in particular),[3] and which he returns to parody here. Heraldry is a

---

3.   See my article "'Heads and Maidenheads': Blasons et contre-blasons du corps dans *Roméo et Juliette*" in Jean-Marie Maguin et Charles Whitworth, eds., *Roméo et Juliette: Nouvelles perspectives critiques*, Collection *Astræa* n° 5, Montpellier, 1993.

miniaturised inventory, an art of detail, to use Daniel Arasse's term.[4] But this time the procedure has an ironic role, as it serves to point out the short-sightedness of Phoebe, who dwells on the part without seeing the whole, that is, the sexual identity of Ganymede. As for Orlando, he had taken the opposite position in one of his poems, borrowing from various divine or symbolic figures the elements of an ideal body or corpus:

> Nature presently distilled
> Helen's cheek, but not her heart,
>   Cleopatra's majesty,
>   Atalanta's better part,
>   Sad Lucretia's modesty.
> Thus Rosalind of many parts
>   By heavenly synod was devised
> Of many faces, eyes, and hearts
>   To have the touches dearest prized. (3.2.139-46)

By instinct, Orlando has seen correctly: Rosalind is one figure of multiplicity in a comedy containing many. The details of her anatomy must therefore be declined in the plural. At the same time, this game gives rise to a somewhat ironic commentary from Rosalind, who laughs with Celia over the rough and rather stumbling poetic activity of the bashful lover in the Forest of Arden:

> CELIA   Didst thou hear these verses?
> ROSALIND   O yes, I heard them all, and more, too, for some of them had in them more feet than the verses would bear.
> CELIA   That's no matter: the feet might bear the verses.
> ROSALIND   Ay, but the feet were lame, and could not bear themselves without the verse, and therefore stood lamely in the verse.
> CELIA   But dist thou hear without wondering how thy name should be *hanged and carved* upon these trees? (3.2.158-67)

The verses are imperfect, the cadence 'lame', but above all, in Celia's mouth, the expression 'hanged and carved' evokes the torture, common at the time, which consisted in hanging a

---

4.   Daniel Arasse, *Le Détail. Pour une histoire rapprochée de la peinture*, Flammarion, Paris, 1992.

condemned person in the public square, then cutting the body in pieces ('hanging and quartering') before dividing up the members. As it happened, the athletic Orlando had fled his paternal home which, according to old Adam, was threatening to become a 'butchery':

> Your brother—no, no brother—...
>   this night he means
> To burn the lodging where you use to lie,
> And you within it. If he fail of that,
> He will have other means *to cut you off.*
> I overheard him and his practices.
> This is no place, this house is but a *butchery.* (2.3.20-28)

If Oliver is a butcher or an ogre to whom Orlando will eventually pay a symbolic blood debt, sustaining an open wound when he fights the lioness barehanded to save him, (4.3.147-49), the lover is less a poet than a Tom Thumb leaving poems on his path in the guise of little white stones. If he tries to reconstruct the body of his beloved with the help of his poetic blazons, Orlando 'innamorato' is pleasantly mocked as someone who lames verses, massacres the name and spoils the trees of the woods, as Jaques points out to him ('I pray you mar no more trees with writing love-songs in their barks,' 2.2.251-52). He is thus ironically presented as an avatar of Sir Oliver *Mar*-text! In the eyes of Jaques, this torturer of hearts is above all the torturer of the trees of the forest, a scandal for a well-intentioned character, whose patronym, justly, is 'de Boys'!

These remarks are among the numerous allusions to music and to the texture of the voice in a play in which ears seem to be very sensitive to dissonance. The forest is a concert of voices in which the slightest discordance, like Jaques's (the Duke describes him as a 'compact of jars,' fearing that he will provoke discord in the cosmic harmony, 2.7.5-6) can cause the whole to go out of tune. But it may also be a question of the love which, if not shared, can turn its object into a mere instrument, such as when Rosalind becomes indignant with a Silvius too easily manipulated by Phoebe:

> What, to make thee an instrument, and play false strains upon thee?
> (4.3.68-69)

The problem in the comedy is not to avoid dissonance, but to isolate and marginalize them, as Jaques does, when he recognizes in the end: 'I am for other than for dancing measures' (5.4.189), before everyone is tuned to the pitch of the collective happiness which triumphs in the *dénouement* of the play. But the collective plighting of troths and marriages in the last act, which Jaques depicts less as the ark of a new alliance than as a Noah's Ark intended to remedy the flood of erotic desires (5.4.35-36), also provide a conventional climax, which, as Anne Barton has noted,[5] presents itself like an artificial finale unashamedly brandishing its arbitrary character. If one can believe Jaques, this Noah's Ark might rapidly turn into a ship of fools.

Indeed in one of his grand scenes, Jaques asks the Duke to let him slip on Harlequin's costume ('I am ambitious for a motley coat,' 2.7.43), to clothe him in this variegated livery ('Invest me in my motley,' l. 58) to permit him to inaugurate the Kingdom of Folly, where he will be the uncontested king. Jaques thus wishes to be the high priest of the Feast of Fools or of what was then called 'l'Abbaye de Maugouvert,' that is, the Abbey of Bad Government (or the equivalent of what is meant in English by 'misrule'),[6] of the upside-down world that was the period of licence or immunity granted to the buffoon during the suspended time of the Feast ('intermission,' l. 32). As the parodic double of the Duke, Jaques intends to be able to discharge his bile freely, to mock whomever he pleases, with relative impunity.

But the real 'Prince of Fools,' 'Abbé des Con(n)ards' or the 'Mère Folle' of this comedy[7] is obviously Touchstone, the true representative of 'nonsense,' the play's grand master of the *non sequitur*, of the inept or incongruous digression. Moreover, he is the model whom Jaques claims as his inspiration. Indeed, Touchstone is a master of the art of improvisation, making

5.   "*As You Like It* and *Twelfth Night*: Shakespeare's Sense of an Ending" (1972) in *Essays, Mainly Shakespearean*, Cambridge University Press, Cambridge, 1994.
6.   See Natalie Zemon Davis, "The Reasons of Misrule" in *Society and Culture in Early Modern France*, Stanford University Press, Stanford, 1965, re-ed. 1975.
7.   Natalie Zemon Davis, "The Reasons of Misrule," pp. 98-99.

speeches that cause the craftiness or the Petrarchianizing inanity of Silvius to explode, Silvius, who, as the crucified lover, manages to draw a sigh from Rosalind by hammering three times on his refrain 'Thou hast not loved':

> I remember when I was in love I broke my sword upon a stone and bid him take that for coming-a-night to Jane Smile, and I remember the kissing of her batlet, and the cow's dugs that her pretty hands had milked; and I remember the wooing of a peascod instead of her, from whom I took two cods, and giving her them again, said with weeping tears, 'Wear these for my sake.' (2.4.43-50)

This facetious litany orchestrated by the series of thrice-repeated 'I remember' echoes Silvius's earlier refrain, as well as Orlando's opening speech, 'As I remember, Adam' (1.1.1). If the pastoral is the school of nostalgia and the *recherche du temps perdu*, the variations of Touchstonian foolishness serve to catalogue the failures, the slips, or the absurdities of amorous behaviour. A parody of the gallant Roland, Touchstone has broken his sword on the Roncevaux of desire; at the same time that he has broken his word ('sword' inverted to 'words'), he has courted a peascod or made love to a codpiece ('peascod' inverted to 'codpiece'), which serves as a warning and a comical prelude to the reversals and sexual disguises of Rosalind as Ganymede-Rosalind, not to mention the succession of obscene innuendos ('stone' being the slang word for testicles). These linguistic somersaults, these verbal fricassees will become a veritable killing game when the fool attacks rustic characters like Corin and William or Audrey, before whom he will deploy the whole gamut of his sparkling and nimble, but also dirty-minded wit. The jester, as Rosalind suggests, is a dangerous fartomaniac[8] ('Thou loosest thy old smell,' 1.2.98) whose example Jaques intends to follow:

---

8.   For a similar example, see Ben Jonson, *Pleasure Reconciled to Virtue* (1618) in David Lindley ed., *Court Masques. Jacobean and Caroline Entertainments 1605-1640*, Oxford University Press, Oxford, 1995, p. 118:
>   BOWL-BEARER   There is no certainty upon Venter, he will blow you all up, he will thunder indeed, la. Some in derision call him the father of farts. But I say he was the first inventor of great ordnance and taught to discharge them in festival days' (ll. 52-56).

> And in his brain,
> . . . he hath strange places crammed
> With observation, the which he *vents*
> In mangled forms . . .
> . . . I must have liberty
> Withal, as large a charter as the *wind*,
> To blow on whom I please, for so fools have . . . (2.7.38-49)

The folly that blows through the forest like the Northern wind in winter is also linked to the idea of carnival and the movement of the winds. Indeed, the humorous etymology of the word 'folly,' going back to the Latin *follis*, meaning 'bellows,' made it possible to associate the swollen bladder of the fool with the bellows of the Mère Folle or with the carnivalesque bum-blowers of the bachelors' clubs or Joyous Societies of the fifteenth century.[9] In this perspective, the friendly brotherhood that surrounds the Duke in exile in the Forest of Arden is less an academy, as in *Love's Labour's Lost*, to whom *As You Like It* is sometimes compared, than a Brotherhood or Abbey of Maugouvert (Bad Government). Juliet Dusinberre has perceptively linked this joyous microcosm with Rabelais' 'Abbaye de Thélème,' whose motto, appropriately, was '*Fay ce que voudras*'.[10] As it happens, the Abbaye de Thélème and the Abbey de Maugouvert were probably linked in the mind of the great connoisseur of carnival and popular culture who was François Rabelais. In both, the cheerful banter of youth was expressed in motley colours of sounds and meanings.

But *As You Like It* also recalls those essays in the forrn of arabesques that Montaigne produced during the course of his intellectual life, like so many glosses or *marginalia* made upon reading or listening to others, and about which he speculated in a somewhat jaded manner:

---

9.   See in this connection Claude Gaignebet et Marie-Claude Florentin, *Le carnaval*, Payot, Paris, 1974, pp. 15, 117-18, et Claude Gaignebet, *A Plus Hault Sens*, 2 vol., Maisonneuve et Larose, Paris, 1986, I, pp. 87-89.
10.   "As *Who* Liked It," *Shakespeare Quarterly* n° 46, *Shakespeare and Sexuality*, Cambridge University Press, Cambridge, 1994, pp. 11-12.

> Que sont-ce icy, à la vérité, que crotesques et corps monstrueux,
> rappiecez de divers membres, sans certaine figure, n'ayants ordre, suite
> ny proportion que fortuite?[11]

At the close of the sixteenth century, the fashion was for those caprices of ornamention imported from Italy, figuring fabulous and surprising interlaced work of vegetables and animals, human figures, masks and minerals, forming monsters or hybrids of a new variety. André Chastel, in the work he devoted to what he proposes calling, in the Italian manner, 'the grottesque,' describes them by analogy with forms of literary buffoonery:

> La référence au coq-à-l'âne, à la contrepèterie, au calembour, à
> l'énumération hagarde, au *lusus verborum* peut nous éclairer. Bref, la
> grottesque refuse la description, et il faut recourir au phénomène
> littéraire parallèle dont la littérature des XVe et XVIe siècles a fait le
> plein : la fatrasie, le macaronique, la fête burlesque du langage.[12]

Grotesques were used to decorate borders, margins, angles or spyholes and, as when carved on Gothic capitals or stalls, they made possible the blossoming and sometimes the unbridling of the imagination of the artists. These are creative whims, the series of criss-crossed and comical images made of fish swimming vertically, hilarious sileni on plinths ending in plants or scrolls, fountains adorned with nymphs spitting water from every orifice, satyrs aiming their arrows at the curves of a callipygian anatomy, or elephants with feet tapering to become reeds. Clearly these fantasies are intended to defy the laws of gravity that rule the ordinary world, and to give birth to all sorts of monsters and chimeras. In a work devoted to them, Philippe Morel gives the example of the English figures from the Ormesby Psalter:

> [Il] nous montre . . . trois figures hybrides et bien armées, au corps mi-
> humain mi-animal, en train de menacer des petites bêtes inoffensives,
> un escargot, un papillon et un écureuil . . . Cette agressivité du rinceau,
> ce corps à corps de l'animal et du végétal, ou de l'animal avec lui-

---

11. I.28.
12. André Chastel, *La Grottesque. Essai sur l'"ornement sans nom,"* Paris, Editions du Promeneur, 1988, p. 55.

même, entraînent des phénomènes de polymorphisme, d'enchaînement ou d'entrelacs qui se rattachent à la tradition spécifiquement anticlassique de l'initiale enluminée . . . [13]

The author, examining what he calls the 'language of the grotesques,' distinguishes between four types of hybrid figures: anthropomorphic characters (mythological monsters), zoomorphs (crosses between land and marine animals), phytomorphs (monsters with vegetal features) and teratomorphs (monsters with bizarre forms). *As You Like It* uses a rich bestiary, becoming a kind of fable in which animals and human beings exchange places or move back and forth in a system of designation deriving now from heraldic or emblematic usage (the stag), now from the pastoral (the sheep), now from satire (the snail), the carnival (horned beasts), sentimentalisation (the doe and her fawn according to Orlando), now from fantasy (the rat or the Irish wolf for Rosalind), or again, from hodge-podge... As for Touchstone, he amuses himself by confusing 'Goths,' 'goats,' and 'gods,' in a learned play on words associating the exile of Ovid, the poet of the *Metamorphoses* and a caprine herd, once again with the adjective 'capricious' playing on the Latin 'caper,' meaning goat. Touchstone is a learned fool, and his ovine witticisms take the form of Ovidian variations on the central theme of metamorphosis and metempsychosis, in a green world which seems destined for hybridization as much as for the proliferation of forms. A detailed inventory of the zoomorphic images in the play shows that corresponding to each character are one or several totemic, heraldic or satiric signifiers (the injured stag for the Old Duke, the weasel for Jaques, the ox for Orlando, the bird for Rosalind and Celia, the snake for Silvius, etc.). But, marked as the world of comedy is by instability, these images are circulated and interchanged, and constantly being reversed, so that their general or particular meaning is uncertain or scrambled. Rosalind is the one who elaborates her transformations with the most prolixity:

_____

13. Philippe Morel, *Les grotesques. Les figures de l'imaginaire dans la peinture italienne de la fin de la Renaissance*, Flammarion, Paris, 1997, pp. 16-17.

> I will be more jealous of thee than a Barbary cock-pigeon over his hen, more clamorous than a parrot against rain, more new-fangled than an ape, more clamourous in my desires than a monkey. I will weep for nothing, like Diana in the fountain, and I will do that when you are disposed to be merry. I will laugh like a hyena, and that when thou art inclined to sleep (4.1.136-43).

From pigeon to hyena, from prey to predator, from flying to semi-aerial creatures (the monkey) and then to quadrupeds, Ganymede-Rosalind plays here with all the facets of capriciousness and contrariness. The apparently gratuitous analogies follow one another at the mercy of moods more than according to laws or correspondences ruled by the degrees of belonging or suitability in the chain of being. But there is more. In comparing herself by turns to Diana, then to a hyena, she is not content just to place back to back ugliness and beauty, chastity and lewdness; the affinities between 'Diana' and 'hyena' are in fact of an acoustic nature, and form a two-sided medallion, a sort of anamorphosis obeying not the laws of perspective, but those of the crazy clock which seems to govern the unpredictable moods that assimilate her to the cruel Angelica of Ariosto's *Orlando Furioso*, thereby leading her lover to despair and madness. Nor is Rosalind stingy with phytomorphic images, since she compares Touchstone to a medlar tree, with a play on words on 'meddler' or Orlando to a 'dropped acorn.' Her imagination is even keener when, pressing Celia to reveal the identity of the mysterious poet who is carving her name in the trees of the forest, she compares her friend to a bottle whose cork she wishes to pry from the bottle:

> I would thou couldst stammer, that thou mightst pour this concealed man out of thy mouth as wine comes out of a narrow-mouthed bottle— either too much at once, or none at all. I prithee, take the cork out of thy mouth, that I may drink thy tidings. (3.2.192-96)

Here we leave the sphere of the grotesques to rejoin that of the anti-masque (see the bottle-men of Pleasure Reconciled to Virtue)[14] or French court ballet. A similar image occurs in the

---

14. See the description of the play by Orazio Busino, chaplain of the Venetian Embassy in London:

next scene, when Jaques compares the future union of Audrey and Touchstone to two planks of green wood that have been worked upon, and whose wood panelling now has 'play.' We have moved from the world of the forest to the world of elaborately-worked wood, the material artisans use for transformation and marquetry.

> Get you to church, and have a good priest that can tell you what marriage is. This fellow will but join you together as they join wainscot; then one of you will prove a shrunk panel and, like green timber, warp, warp (3.3.78-80).

Other fantasies or verbal variations such as 'bubble reputation' (2.7.152), and 'I answer you right painted cloth' (3.2.265) take their lexicon from the craftsmanship of the glass-blowers and tapestry-makers, and evoke the popular professions of engraving, of proverbs, or of court ballet.[15] This world can be seen in the proverbial sayings of the Epilogue: ('To good wine they do use good bushes' or 'I am not furnished like a beggar'), where words and things are brought together, paired, with the help of tokens and labels, the way the male sex is associated with the wearing of a beard and femininity with sweet breath. This is because, upon emerging from the confusions of identity and the sexual, imaginary and linguistic confusions of the forest, that overgrown area of variegation, of metamorphosis, and even anamorphosis, where being and appearing, word and essence appear to be confounded, it seems necessary to establish a fresh, quasi-nominalistic foundation.

If Arden is indeed an enchanted world, it is somewhat in the manner of the Wonderland of Lewis Carroll. Here Shakespeare, instead of holding a mirror up to nature as he does, or says he is

---

Then followed twelve extravagant masquers, one with a barrel round his middle, the others in great wicker flasks very well made . . .
in Christopher Edwards ed., *The London Theatre Guide 1576-1642*, Burlington Press, Cambridge, 1979, p. 50.
15.   See in Particular Marie-Francoise Christout, *Le Ballet de Cour au XVIIe siècle*, Editions Minkoff, Genève, 1987, p. 67 (plate n° 47 representing a Caster in the chapter entitled "Du réel au burlesque").

doing, in *Hamlet*, leads us around to the other side of the mirror, to the land of madness, where words are ripped from their habitual, accepted meanings in order to freely express desire, delirium, fantasy, and incongruous associations like those in the pictorial world of the grotesques. This 'Sotie' or 'Fatrasie' that he plants in the middle of the green world is a place enamelled with quotations and reminiscences, with subtle resonances and secret correspondences, as much as with the logic or with the motley variations of meanings at the mercy of reasonings, recitations or disputes that are given free rein, or are offered as a spectacle before an audience that is clamouring for more.

The sparkling contortions of language are based on the reversibility of worlds and forms, on the permeability of front and back, on desires, whims or moods, and they make of this play a prototype of the 'Comedy of Wit.' Sense and nonsense, absurdity and irrefutable logic are interchanged at the whims of the hypotheses, possibilities, and wanderings of heart and mind. Two magic letters must thus be added in capital letters to this comedy of the free exchange, of invention, but also of translation and conversion, namely: 'IF,' the magic key which makes it possible to combine dream and reality. It is at one and the same time what opens the doors of the imaginary, and the wager that makes this act possible. It is in the name of this double principle that the structure of this comedy in *trompe-l'œil* takes shape, at once parody and 'pot pourri,' a necessarily eclectic work, as the title indicates, but equally dizzying in its stunning practice of theatrical 'mise en abyme' and its play on the multiple deviations and bifurcations of meaning.

François LAROQUE

IV. 'So quiet and so sweet a style' (2.1.20) The Style of the Eclogue and the Praise of Style

A world of cross-dressing, of conversion, of transition, of exile, of the transfer of inheritance, of translation and self-translation, *As You Like It* seems to be a dramatic variation on the notion of 'translation,' which, according to Amiens, defines the easily identifiable pastoral style articulated by the exiled Duke:

> Happy is your Grace,
> That can translate the stubbornness of fortune
> Into so quiet and so sweet a style. (2.1.18-20)

This commentary on style is linked—grafted, as it were—to a spontaneous utterance of praise: Amiens's praise for the Duke's own speech in praise of nature not only raises the obvious question of artifice, but also anticipates such present-day preoccupations as the status of language, the translation of classical texts, the stylistic choices available to pastoral comedy, the relationship between image and speech, and the limits of interpretation. The polysemy of the two principal terms ('translate' and 'style') provides the four lines of exploration offered here.

First, 'style' will be examined in its primary meaning, as an engraver's tool ('stylus'); then 'translation' will be considered in its first category of meaning, writing, and in particular, in the relationship which writing establishes between body and text. The text of *As You Like It*, even in the burlesque mode, provides an echo of the debate which runs throughout the Renaissance,[1]

---

1. See in this connection: Pico della Mirandola. *Conclusiones, sive theses DCCC.* Romae, 1486, re-ed. in *Travaux d'Humanisme et Renaissance* n° 131, ed. Bohdan Kieszkowski, Geneva, Droz, 1973, p. 73.
Marsilo Ficino, *Argumentum in Cratylum, vel de recta nominum ratione. Opera omnia,* Basel, 1586, II, ii.

on the natural or arbitrary[2] character of the linguistic sign, and leads to that magical reading of the world referred to by Michel Foucault in his chapter on 'the prose of the world' in *Les Mots et les Choses*.[3] A world of naming, of oaths and of rituals, the Forest of Arden is also a world of nicknames, of interrupted ceremonies and of broken promises; a place where writing is violence and reading is a form of torture. The style here is a point of sharpened steel, fine line or scalpel stroke, whether it strips the bark from the trees or dissects the body politic.

The second type of 'translation' to be considered here is that of cross-dressing and the lie. *As You Like It* celebrates and praises the lie and the rhetoric of the lie as much as it uses its sexual equivalent, transvestism, as its most powerful dramatic tool. Arden is a linguistic universe whose syntax is in the conditional: the entire difference in meaning rests upon the two letters of the conjunction 'if,' which constitute the thickness of the diaphanous veil that separates the hypothetical from the real. The mediating role of the discourse, the presence of barely veiled enigmas, the exposition of the artifice and the theatrical character of language itself constitute the elements of this discursive 'translation' of the real.

A third approach to the reading will be in the area of translation, understood both as interpretation or passage from one language to another, or from one level of language to another, and as relation between image and discourse. One of the questions raised by this particular scene of course, is how images speak, and how dramatic discourse distributes and integrates them. In this case, it is the moralised play in its emblematic dimension that presents the greatest problem for interpretation.

---

2.   See in particular: Keir Elam, *Shakespeare's Universe of Discourse. Language-Games in the Comedies*, Cambridge: Cambridge University Press, 1984, pp. 116-76. See also Pierre Iselin, "'What shall I swear by?' Rhetoric and Attitudes to Language in *Romeo and Juliet*," in *'Divers toyes mengled': Essays on Medieval and Renaissance Culture, In honour of André Lascombes*, Publications de l'Université François Rabelais-Tours, 1996, pp. 261-280.

3.   Michel Foucault, *Les Mots et les Choses*, Paris: Gallimard, 1966, ch. II, pp. 32-60.

Finally, the most complex forms of translation to be considered will involve relations of exchange, inversion, opposition or imitation. Here it will be a question of the hybridization of styles, of discourse on style, and of the plurality of voices.

The style, in its definition as instrument, is aggressive: a hard point, it must carve, engrave, mark. The writing, therefore, is a scar, and reading opens wounds. Thus the fictitious trees of the imaginary Forest of Arden undergo a sophisticated process of grafting, which produces fruits of uncertain definition:[4] It is love songs that Orlando pins there, or the name he carves, reproducing mechanically, and thus comically, the ancient, now stereotypical, gesture of the Virgilian lover.[5]

> certum est in silvis, inter spelaea ferarum
> malle pati tenerisque meos incidere amores
> arboribus: crescent illae, crescetis, amores.[6]

The meeting of Jaques and Orlando, who play respectively the roles of Mar-tree and Mar-text, places on an equal footing the operations of reading and writing, which are both associated with violence:

> JAQUES   I pray you mar no more trees with writing love songs in their barks.
> ORLANDO   I pray you mar no more of my verses with reading them ill-favouredly. (3.2.251-54)

The repetition of the act and the multiplication of the poems emerge as objects of a discourse which is itself repetitive, since

---

4.   3.2.111-18.
5.   See in particular the episode of Angelica and Medoro in Ariosto's *Orlando Furioso*, quoted in Brissenden, *op. cit.*, p. 155.
6.   Virgil, Eclogue X.
[it is certain that in the forest, among the caves of the wild beasts, it is better to suffer and carve my love on the young trees: when they grow, you will grow, my love.] Quoted in Thomas McFarland, *Shakespeare's Pastoral Comedy*, Chapel Hill: The University of North Carolina Press, p. 113.

three references are made to it,[7] the most striking being an image offered by Rosalind a little later:

> There is a man haunts the forest that abuses our young plants with carving 'Rosalind' on their barks; hangs odes upon hawthorns and elegies on brambles; all, forsooth, deifying the name of Rosalind. (3.2.343-46)

The scorn is aimed as much at the proliferation of these writings as at the particular form of idolatry the deification of the name inevitably brings to mind: this cult of the linguistic sign, here treated in the ironic mode, is nonetheless the echo of a conception of language in the Renaissance; even if the Orphic definition is not the only discourse on language in the English Renaissance,[8] it is nonetheless the dominant discourse. The debate on the sign, natural or arbitrary, underlies several of Shakespeare's plays, whether in speculations about connections between name and person or between literal and tropological meanings, or in proposals for a reading of the world as a text to be deciphered. It is the metaphor of the book which orients the pastoral discourse of the exiled Duke; the same metaphor transforms the forest into a library and trees into books, or rather, notebooks, for the apprentice poet-lover Orlando. When the Duke turns the world into a book of Stoic wisdom, the metaphor is approved by Amiens, who praises its poetic and moral character (the style transforms the perception of adversity and sweetens it). On the contrary, the hypostatic form of it that Orlando exhibits borders on the ridiculous, like his hyperbolic vows ('for ever and a day'). It is clear that the Ficinian intertext is praised, while the Virgilian pose of the lover/tree-carver is treated with derision. The same conception of language, however, informs the two attitudes.

---

7.   The third reference is an allusion to grafting, in an equivocal exchange between Touchstone and Rosalind:
      ROSALIND   Peace, you dull fool, I found them under a tree.
      TOUCHSTONE   Truly, the tree yields bad fruit.
      ROSALIND   I'll graft it with you, and then I'll graft it with a medlar; . . . (3.2.110-14)
8.   See Elam, *ibid.*

The literary motif of the tree, which the rhetoric of treatises baptised 'dendographia,' is sufficiently present in the play to warrant a brief analysis. In Shakespeare's comedy, in which not only texts but also interpretations proliferate, the tree is the synecdoche of the forest, the haunt of exiles, the place where Jaques lies down to observe the spectacle of the wounded stag, and where Oliver, restored to his natural state, is observed by his brother and by a lioness lying in wait; for Touchstone, it is also the fraudulent alternative to church, for Amiens, the background for a bucolic song ('Under the Greenwood Tree'); more generally, the tree provides the foundation for metaphors expressing themes of growth, pruning and grafting. As an element in a fictitious scene, subjected to the alterations and the play of meanings related to antanaclasis, it is for Orlando the material grounds for the writing of amorous desire:

> O Rosalind, these trees shall be my books,
>   And in their barks my thoughts I'll character
> That every eye which in this forest looks
>   Shall see thy virtue witnessed everywhere.
> Run, run, Orlando; carve on every tree
> The fair, the chaste, and unexpressive she. (3.2.5-10)

The truncated sonnet the lover reads is the literal, burlesque counterpoint of the bucolic and Orphic discourse enunciated earlier by the Duke, who had turned the tree into a hieroglyph in which the signatures so dear to Crollius could be discerned:

> And this our life, exempt from public haunt,
> Finds tongues in trees, books in the running brooks,
> Sermons in stones, and good in everything. (2.1.15-17)

As it happens, the metaphorical fangs and bites ('icy fangs,' 'bites and blows upon my body'), become literal at Orlando's expense, under another tree, at the time of his struggle with the lioness.

In the same way, language materializes when Phoebe's missive is submitted to a brutal graphic analysis:

> ROSALIND   I say she never did invent this letter:
> This is a man's invention, and his hand.
> SILVIUS   Sure, it is hers.

> ROSALIND   Why, 'tis a boisterous and a cruel style,
> A style for challengers. Why, she defies me,
> Like Turk to Christian. (4.3.29-33)

The style here is stiletto, and the billet doux a duellist's challenge. The writing in it is at one and the same time disguise and aggression. Similarly, by distorting Phoebe's declaration, the reading disguises and misrepresents by turn, making violence the key to any possible decoding. The suggestion that the writing is the result of a sexualized transvestism ('his hand'), in which the body appears implicitly, emanates from Rosalind-as-Ganymede; sartorial transvestism and epistolary tranvestism are thus placed in a situation full of ironic echoes. The reality of the body, however, is in each case seen through the diaphanous veil of the artifice. Arden, this space of disguising and naming, sees Rosalind take the name of Ganymede, the mythical model of transvestism, debased as a 'catamite,' while Celia takes the name of Aliena, which suits her state of alienation:

> CELIA   What shall I call thee when thou art a man?
> ROSALIND   I'll have no worse a name than Jove's own page,
> And therefore look you call me Ganymede.
> But what will you be called?
> CELIA   Something that hath a reference to my state.
> No longer Celia, but Aliena. (1.3.122-27)

This indicates that within the world of the play, the choice of names is purposeful, and even influences the world of ordinary language.[9]

An absent signifier unites the three stylistic registers of style, forest and magic: it is the uncle with whom Rosalind identifies for his linguistic competence and an unknown character for his knowledge of magic. The association of language and magic is achieved via these two fictitious professors, whom Orlando

---

9.   No doubt the characteristic example is 'she Phoebes me' (4.3.30), which constitutes a 'mise en abyme': of the pastoral style, in which Rosalind has the conventional role of the haughty shepherdess. See also the word-play on 'whetstone,' 'Rose,' 'Martext,' and the onomastics even of the names 'Orlando,' 'Oliver,' 'DuBoys,' etc.

interprets as one single character (5.4.32). Elsewhere, the magical relationship between word and thing is illustrated by Rosalind's amused comment when she discovers her name engraved or exhibited on the trees:

> CELIA   Didst thou hear these verses?
> ROSALIND   O yes, I heard them all, and more too, for some of them had in them more feet than the verses would bear.
> CELIA   That's no matter; the feet might bear the verses.
> ROSALIND   Ay, but the feet were lame, and could not bear themselves without the verse, and therefore stood lamely in the verse.
> CELIA   But didst thou hear without wondering how thy name should be hanged and carved upon these trees?
> ROSALIND   I was seven of the nine days out of the wonder before you came; for look here what I found on a palm-tree; *(showing Celia the verses)* I was never so berhym'd since Pythagoras' time that I was an Irish rat, which I can hardly remember. (3.2.158-72)

While the first part of the dialogue finds fault with the metrics of Orlando's blazoning poem, and pronounces on the nature of 'feet' in the passage from text to body, the second part treats this same passage in the mode of the poem of invective. Here are the ancient origins of the reputedly murderous iamb, and that form of gaelic poetry attested by the proverb,[10] as well as by Philip Sidney[11] and Ben Jonson:

> I could do worse,
> Arm'd with Archilocus fury, write Iambics,
> Should make the desperate lashers hang themselves.
> Rime 'em to death, as they do Irish rats
> In drumming tunes.[12]

The *vis verborum* is specifically evoked by Rosalind when she refers to Pythagoras, citing his theory of metempsychosis, as

---

10.   M. P. Tilley, *A Dictionary of the Proverbs in England in the Sixteenth and Seventeenth Centuries*, Ann Arbor, 1950, D158. Quoted in a note in the World's Classics edition, ed. Alan Brissenden, The Oxford Shakespeare, Oxford: Oxford University Press, 1993, p. 164.
11.   Philip Sidney, *A Defence of Poetry*: 'not to be rhymed to death, as is said to be done in Ireland' (ed. J. van Dorsten, Oxford, 1966, p. 75).
12.   Ben Jonson, *The Poetaster*, 'Apologetical Dialogue,' ll. 160-164, ed. C. H. Herford and Percy Simpson, Vol. IV, Oxford: Clarendon Press, 1932. Quoted by Agnes Latham, in The Arden Shakespeare, London: Methuen, 1975, p. 69.

reported by Ovid in Book V of *Metamorphoses*.[13] The reference to the Irish rat is thus a would-be ironic allusion to the power of poetic and musical ritual, and therefore to the definition of language as magic. 'Translation' here takes on the meaning of metamorphosis, as in the formula: 'Bottom, thou art translated!'

Confusion between the name and the thing can result in other comic metamorphoses, as when, for example, impatient to know the identity of the poet who is celebrating her, Rosalind confuses the name and the person, making of the person a cork stuck in her cousin's mouth:

> I would thou could'st stammer, that thou mightst pour this conceal'd man out of thy mouth, as wine comes out of narrow-mouth'd bottle— either too much at once or none at all. I prithee take the cork out of thy mouth that I may drink thy tidings. (3.2.192-96)

The pastoral vision, references to the Golden Age, the presence on the scene of an Adam, reveal between the lines of comic

_____

13. Heere dwelt a man of Samos Ile, who for the hate he had
    Too Lordlynesse and Tyranny, though unconstrayned was glad
    Too make himself a bannisht man . . .
    He also is the first that did injoyne an abstinence
    Too feede of any living thing . . .
                        Oh what a wickednesse
    It is to cram the mawe with mawe, and frank up flesh with flesh,
    And for one living thing too live of another . . .
                        But that same auncient age
    Which wee have naamed the golden worlde, cleene voyd of all such
                                            rage,
    Livd blessedly by frute of trees and herbes that grow on ground,
    And stayned not their mouthes with blood . . .
                        But after that the lust
    Of one (what God so ere he was) disdeyning former fare,
    Too cram that cruell croppe of his fleshmeate did not spare,
    He made a way for wickednesse. And first of all the knyfe
    Was stayned with blood of savage beastes in ridding them of lyfe . . .
    What trespasse have the Oxen doone, a beaste without all guyle,
    Or craft, unhurtfull, simple, borne too labour every whyle? . . .
                        But give good eare and heede
    Too that that I shall warn you of, and trust it as your creede,
    That whensoever you doo eate your Oxen, you devowre
    Your husbandmen. (Ovid, *Metamorphoses*, Golding, trans.)

discourse the notion of the *lingua adamica*, the language of
origins, a 'natural' translation of landscape into language. It can
be seen that the relationship between language and landscape
set forth by the Duke is a mutual one, since Nature's speech is
addressed to him:

> Here feel we not the penalty of Adam,
> The seasons' difference, as the icy fang
> And churlish chiding of the winter's wind,
> Which when it bites and blows upon my body
> Even till I shrink with cold, I smile and say
> 'This is no flattery. These are *counsellors*
> That feelingly *persuade me* what I am.' (2.1.5-11)

The speech *about* Nature thus appears to be fed by a discourse
by Nature, the mutual relationship providing the basis for the
pastoral style praised by Amiens, and whose comic
reverberations in the play are numerous. This praise of the
eclogue, incidentally, gives to the style an implicitly ethical
definition, because such a manner of speaking is at the same
time a manner of being, in this case a way of reacting to the
strokes of fortune. The style, like 'wit,' that gift of nature
celebrated by Rosalind (1.2) or by Jaques,[14] is the antidote to
the vicissitudes of life. But this reading of the world, as Amiens
suggests, is at once biased and incomplete: rendering the world
of nature only in 'beneficial' mode ('good in everything'), such a
personal translation is deceptive. As it happens, it is not the only
encomium of the lie associated with style: Jaques encores
Touchstone's elaborate speech on the seven degrees of the lie
(5.4.84-85), while the love cure is based on a deceptive illusion
entered into willingly. The truth is thus glimpsed only fleetingly,
through the mode of paradox and ambiguity:

> ORLANDO   Fair youth, I would I could make thee believe I love.
> ROSALIND   Me believe it? You may as soon make her that you love
> believe it, which I warrant she is apter to do than to confess she does.
> (3.2. 367-71)

---

14.   JAQUES You have a nimble wit; I think 'twas made of Atalanta's heels. Will you sit
down with me? and we two will rail against our mistress the world, and all our misery.
(3.2.267-70)

Here truth is hidden in a deliberately ambiguous syntax, whose periphrastic and anaphoric constructions promote doubt, when the enigma could be solved by a simple substitution of pronouns. The game of hypothesis serves to mediate the discourse on identity: language, then, takes on an eminently theatrical function, since it is the very syntax itself which deceives, just as Rosalind's masculine accoutrements turn Orlando into a kind of dupe in a panoptic situation. Kept in ignorance, and sometimes observed without his knowledge, Orlando is unable to decode the signs—and even winks—which Rosalind addresses to her two publics: Celia on the one hand, and the knowing spectator on the other. This exercise in virtuosity, in which truth and lies flirt on the surface of the discourse, brings to mind another panegyric of style-as-lie, Touchstone's praise of poetry:

> AUDREY   I do not know what 'poetical' is. Is it honest in deed and word? Is it a true thing?
> TOUCHSTONE No, truly; for the truest poetry is the most feigning, and lovers are given to poetry; and what they swear in poetry it may be said, as lovers, they do feign. (3.3.14-18)

The polysemy of 'feign' ('invent' and 'lie') causes the jester to say two things at once, amounting to an admission that his definition of the lie in poetry, a subject debated and re-debated from Plato to Philip Sidney,[15] is founded on a lie. And then, in a supreme hyperbole from the very champion of Petrarchan hyperbole, the incapacity of poetic language to speak truth, and thus to express passion, is denied:

> ROSALIND   But are you so much in love as your rhymes speak?
> ORLANDO   Neither rhyme nor reason can express how much.
> (3.2.377-80)

The most histrionic of the tropes, the one Puttenham translated with the theatrical term 'overreacher,'[16] reduces the totality of the artifices of language to the single term 'rhyme,' which, like

---

15.   Philip Sidney, *op. cit.*, pp. 52-53.
16.   George Puttenham, *The Arte of English Poesie*, London, 1589, fol. 159, repr. E. Arber, London, 1859, p. 202.

the proverb, he opposes to 'reason.' As deceitful and artificial as it may be, poetic language still remains on this side of passion. This is how the paradox of the true lie, the authentic artifice, and the euphemistic hyperbole may be articulated: passion exceeds excess; any effort to translate it will always be unfaithful to the original. Although commentaries on language in *As You Like it* are recurrent, and bear on distinct styles (bucolic, amorous, musical), the only critique of poetic style found in Lodge is a long indictment of desire, which, as it happens, recalls the figure of the Latin poet:

> 'I can smile,' quoth Ganymede, 'at the sonettos, canzonas, madrigals, rounds, and roundelays that these pensive patients pour out when their eyes are more full of wantonness than their hearts of passion. Then, as the fishers put the sweetest bait to the fairest fish, so theses Ovidians (holding *amo* in their tongues when their thoughts come at haphazard) write that they be wrapt in an endless labyrinth of sorrow, when walking in the large leas of liberty, they only have their humors in their inkpot. If they find women so fond that they will with such painted lures come to their lust, then they triumph till they be gorged with pleasures, and then fly they away like ramage kites to their own content, leaving the tame fool; their mistress, full of fancy yet without ever a feather. If they miss, as dealing with some wary wanton that wants not such a one as themselves, but spies their subtlety, they end their amours with a few feigned sighs, and so their excuse is their mistress is cruel and they smother passions with patience.[17]

While in Lodge, the critique of style and poetic genre is reduced to this single retort from Ganymede, stylistic criticism in *As You Like It* is a counter-discourse that tends to overrun the play, and is the monopoly of no one in particular: Amiens, Touchstone, but also Celia, Rosalind and Jaques, are trained stylists, who judge figures of speech and give diagnostic studies of metre, including one isolated occurrence of pentameter:

> ORLANDO Good day and happiness, dear Rosalind!
> JAQUES   Nay, then, Goodbye an you talk in blank verse. (4.1.28-29)

---

17. Thomas Lodge, *Rosalind*, ed. Donald Beecher, Ottawa: Dovehouse Editions, 1997, p. 160.

This attention to stylistic detail offers a rolling train of metadiscursive remarks, giving to poetic artifice the status of a general framework. While Lodge gives free rein to poetic discourse inserted without ironic or parodic distance into dramatic exchanges or narrative text, Shakespeare turns his pastoral play into a reflection on style: when a poetic idiom is identified, it is immediately treated either in contestation mode, or in imitation mode. In the stylistic universe of *As You Like It*, what is not contrasted is parodied. In this way, the style of the eclogue is never presented as such, but emerges as an element of the scene, 'mis en abyme' in the eavesdropping scenes, before becoming an object of discourse. Style as an aspect of the spectacle and an aspect of discourse reverses the connection between the frame and the logic of the emblem: it is not the discourse which frames and elucidates the image, but the poetic discourse which becomes the framed object of speculation.

This pattern relates in particular to the recurrent image of the stag. As Michael Bath[18] has rightly noted, an iconographic reading here presents more problems than it solves. Jaques seems at first to identify with the injured stag, a spectacle to which he gives a thousand moral interpretations:

> DUKE SENIOR But what said Jaques?
> Did he not moralize this spectacle?
> FIRST LORD O, yes, into a thousand similes.
> First, for his weeping into the needless stream;
> 'Poor deer,' quoth he, 'thou mak'st a testament
> As worldlings do, giving thy sum of more
> To that which had too much.' Then, being there alone,
> Left and abandoned of his velvet friend,
> ''Tis right,' quoth he, 'thus misery doth part
> The flux of company.' Anon, a careless herd
> Full of the pasture jumps along by him
> And never stays to greet him. 'Ay,' quoth Jaques,
> 'Sweep on, you fat and greasy citizens,
> 'Tis just the fashion. Wherefore do you look
> Upon that poor and broken bankrupt there?' (2.1.45-57)

---

18. Michael Bath, 'Weeping Stags and Melancholy Lovers: The Iconography of *As You Like It*,' *Emblematica*, 1 (1986): 13-52.

In the face of the proliferation of these allegorical interpretations, all proceeding from anthropomorphism, how can a reading, as a process of univocal decoding, be envisaged? One cannot help noticing a radical change in Jaques's attitude during the hunting ritual which celebrates the death of the stag. Is there not in Jaques, as in Duke Senior, the same need to interpret the natural spectacle according to contrasting 'styles'? It is of note that the interpretive act (Jaques moralising on the living image of the stag) is related here by an anonymous narrator ('First Lord'), which makes it even less immediate, and this even less so because to interpret, Jaques must, as it were, enter the scene he is commenting upon: first through the personal identification of a Jaques-Narcissus, weeping, like the stag, at the edge of the stream, then in an anthropomorphic projection. Interpreting is thus a specular activity, as is suggested by the pleasantry about the painting of 'We Three' in *Twelfth Night*.[19] The painting depicts only two donkeys, when the title has announced three: if the spectator recognizes himself in the third, it is because he accepts his asinine status; if he refuses it, it is because he does not understand the game, and is thus implicitly reduced to the same status ('reader, thou art translated!'). The problem of interpretation, therefore, raises the question of the frame of reference: here, the account frames an animated spectacle, itself interpreted according to the plethoric model of emblematic allegory and the theatrical code of the soliloquy, since, spied upon by the two gentlemen, Jaques moralises aloud on a highly recognizable spectacle from emblematic iconography. From this perspective, one can say with David Young: 'In *As You Like It*, we are invited to view the pastoral convention simultaneously from the inside, as in Lodge, and from the outside, as a frankly artificial and illusory construction.'[20] The pastoral, enclosed within a frame, sometimes interrupted, often subjected to secret inspection, thus appears as a stylised *décor*. The *topographia*, which Puttenham renders as

---

19. See in this connection Elizabeth Freund, '*Twelfth Night* and the Tyranny of Interpretation.' *English Literary History* 53.3 (1986): 471-89.
20. David Young, *The Heart's Forest, A Study of Shakespeare's Pastoral Plays*, New Haven and London: Yale University Press, 1972, p. 70.

'counterfeit place,' intensifies the arcadian spectacle of oak, stag and stream, but the situation of enunciation, by its complexity, indicates the artifice behind it: the topos of contemporary iconography participates in the strategy of *trompe-l'œil*.

The translation of the image, then, presents the problem of artifice and of setting. By evoking Jaques and his hermeneutic soliloquy, the narrator himself interprets an image, since Jaques's posture is easily identifiable according to iconographic codes: it is that of the melancholic in the miniatures of Nicholas Hilliard or Isaac Oliver; but such posture may equally call to mind that of Tityrus, the shepherd of the Virgilian eclogues, stretching out happily in the shade of a beech tree. The same position, in similar surroundings, is taken up again in the temptation scene, when Orlando observes his brother Oliver stretched out at the foot of an oak, at the very moment when Oliver is being observed by a lioness and a serpent has just unwound itself from his neck:[21]

> OLIVER
> Under an oak, whose boughs were moss'd with age,
> And high top bald with dry antiquity,
> A wretched ragged man, o'ergrown with hair,
> Lay sleeping on his back. About his neck
> A green and gilded snake had wreath'd itself,
> Who with her head nimble in threats approach'd
> The opening of his mouth; but suddenly,
> Seeing Orlando, it unlink'd itself,
> And with indented glides did slip away
> Into a bush, (4.3.105-14)

Besides the similitude of the *décor*, it can be seen that the account establishes a whole *mise en scène*, recounted here by the very one who is the object of the spectacle. The only scene in which Orlando spies instead of being spied upon, is, curiously, told by the very object of his spying, Oliver. The account thus diametrically reverses the perspective. The setting for these observations, the framework of the spectacle, the posture made

---

21.   For a detailed allegorical reading of this passage, see Alice-Lyle Scoufos, 'The Paradisio Terrestre and the Testing of Love in *As You Like It*,' *Shakespeare Studies*, 14 (1981), 215-27.

into a spectacle mediated by the account, have the effect of making the two scenes remote, even totally artificial.

Detail equally tends to reverse the perspective of the whole, as for example, when the motif of the tears reproduces in miniature that of the hunt:

> and the big round tears
> Coursed one another down his innocent nose
> In piteous chase. (2.1.38-40)

Not long after this first mirrored inversion, another one occurs, *via* an implied image, that of the arrow and the wound. Jaques the satirist, after having identified himself with the game-animal victim, becomes the archer who shoots his lines into the world, as hunters shoot game:

> Thus most invectively he pierceth through
> The body of the country, city, court,
> Yea, and of this our life, swearing that we
> Are mere usurpers, tyrants, and what's worse,
> To fright the animals and to kill them up
> In their assigned and native dwelling-place. (2.1.58-63)

In an almost mannerist style, detail puts the whole tableau 'en abyme' and inverts its polarities. The motif of the Cervidae appears in two other inversions. Orlando, identifying himself with a doe (2.7.128), interprets old Adam as a 'faun,' subverting by his allegorical commentary the master-servant, old-young, male-female relationships. Later on it is Rosalind who, playing on the 'hart'-'heart' homophony, makes of Orlando the hunter who has come to kill her heart:

> CELIA   ... —He was furnished like a hunter—
> ROSALIND   O ominous—he comes to kill my heart. (3.2.237-38)

In interpreting this description of the clothing and identifying herself with a potential game animal, she who has refuted the Petrarchan idiom[22] has recourse to the conventional metaphor

_____

22.   See in particular 4.1.86-98.

of the amorous chase and the *cliché* of the eye that kills, thereby reversing the traditional roles of lover and mistress.

Another series of images for symbolic and paradoxical decoding constitutes the self-portrait of Ganymede in his role as Rosalind:

> I will be more jealous of thee than a Barbary cock-pigeon over his hen, more clamorous than a parrot against rain, more new-fangled than an ape, more giddy in my desires than a monkey. I will weep for nothing, like Diana in the fountain, and I will do that when you are disposed to be merry. I will laugh like a hyena, and that when thou are inclined to sleep. (4.1.136-43)

This histrionic programme of training, of being broken in, in which it is possible to recognize a reversal of the *Taming of the Shrew* scenario, participates in a logic of the juxtaposition of contraries. As Carroll[23] points out, Rosalind, in clothing herself in the vestments of masculinity, appropriates the masculine discourse on the inconstancy of women. The contagion of styles affects Rosalind as it affects the other characters in the play: linked with the principle of 'translation,' thus of transformation, it provokes the most improbable hybridizations, whether of Jaques sacrificing to the ritual of rhetoric as he pronounces his final benedictions, or of Touchstone proclaiming himself the grand rhetorician in his skirmish of wit against William, or yet again making a pastiche of the style of duelling treatises, or of those voguish ones consecrated to the education of courtisans, of which in particular the most famous was a translation from the Italian.

Nurtured by the styles of other genres, practising in its own stylistic space a hybridization of its different styles, *As You Like It* is a pastoral that feeds on the very questions it raises, because the exercise consists in being distanced from the very style which is supposed to constitute it. An inter- and intra-textual echo chamber, the play juxtaposes, contrasts, quotes, imitates, and thus creates a polyphony of styles in which virtuosity and mockery compete with each other on stage.

Pierre ISELIN

⎯⎯⎯⎯⎯⎯⎯⎯⎯⎯

23.   William C. Carroll, *The Metamorphoses of Shakespearean Comedy*, Princeton: Princeton University Press, 1985, p. 133.

V. Nurture in *As You Like It*

Orlando's initial tirade in *As You Like It*, while verbalizing a personal resentment at the unfair treatment a younger brother receives at the hands of a now omnipotent, father-like, elder brother and the former's legitimate claim articulates the three meanings of a rare term in Shakespeare and elsewhere, 'nurture,' defined by *OED* as follows:

> 1. Breeding, upbringing, training, education (received or possessed by one).
> 2. That which nourishes; nourishment, food.
> 3. The bringing-up or rearing of some one; tutelage; fostering care.

Orlando successively complains about his breeding as compared to that of his brother Jaques, whom Oliver keeps at school; about his food ('he lets me feed with his hinds,' 1.1.17); and about his younger brother's status which he perceives as a servitude ('the spirit of my father, which I think is within me, begins to mutiny against this servitude,' 1.1.20-22).

Not only does Orlando's discourse follow the polysemy of 'nurture' which serves as a sub-text for the whole scene, but it also implicitly voices the conventional debate over the two implicit notions of nature and nurture, as appears in such remarks as: '[he] stays me here at home unkept' (1.1.7-8) or 'the something that nature gave me his countenance seems to take from me' (16-17), '[he] mines my gentility with my education' (19). Far more systematically, Shakespeare's source text, Lodge's *Rosalynde—Rosalind* in the modern-spelling edition of Donald Beecher quoted here—balances the two notions in a typically euphuistic manner. Saladyne's plot against Rosader is expressed in terms similar to Orlando's initial claim: 'though he be a gentleman by nature, yet form him anew and make him a peasant by nurture' (104); later in the temptation scene, Rosader's interior voice reminds the hero of his inherited sense of honor: 'Shall thy nature be so cruel, or thy nurture so crooked . . . ?' (173), and Rosader's forgiveness is heralded by the same pattern of antithesis: 'Rosader, seeing he was unknown to his brother, wondered to hear such courteous words come from his crabbed nature, but glad of such reformed nurture' (174). Shakespeare's canon only counts two occurrences of 'nurture,' one in *As You Like It*, when Orlando justifies his 'smooth civility' in terms of gentle birth (one sense of 'gentility') and polite manners (another sense of 'gentility'): 'Yet am I inland bred, / And know some nurture' (2.7.96-97), the other in *The Tempest*, when Prospero records his failure to educate Caliban 'on whose nature nurture will never stick' (4.1.189). The themes of education, food, and tutelage implied in the notion of nurture—a term derived from the French 'nourriture'—overlap from beginning to end in Shakespeare's play, and characterize not only Orlando's violent claim for education (1.1), food (2.7), and recognition (2.7 and 4.3), but inform the trajectory of the play as a whole.

The nurturing process is at work in Arden, as the notion implies not only culture and food, but also attitude to language, art, and sophistication in all its guises including disguise, in other words what Amiens would call 'translation.' Nurture is not only what is acquired as opposed to what is innate; it is also the force that transforms through a process of education. At the beginning of Act 2, Duke Senior translates the buffets of fortune 'into so quiet and sweet a style' (2.1.20), as if his 'style'—the sophistication of high culture Orlando is after—could be intellectually and ethically operative in the domain of real life, in other words as if nurture could not only interpret and change the world, life and history, but also through a sort of purgation, affect the perception of things and of self, contributing to the Christian and stoic regressive stance of the Duke as pupil, humbly learning his lessons from the book of nature:

> 'This is no flattery. These are counsellors
> That feelingly persuade me what I am.' . . .
> And this our life, exempt from public haunt,
> Finds tongues in trees, books in the running brooks,
> Sermons in stones, and good in everything. (2.1.10-17)

The Duke's poetic diction makes Arden not only rhyme with, but also reflect, Eden, as he claims that 'Here feel we not the penalty of Adam' (5). His spontaneous address and poetical 'translation' of the hardships inherent in the forester's life (2.1.1-17) are recognizably Virgilian: the praise of the wild nature waves an intertextual—*i.e.* cultural—flag for the audience. Besides, all the stock-items of the Lylyan style are conspicuously present (assonances, alliterations, contrasts and carefully devised balances) to assert the main theme of the play, *i.e.* the healing and nurturing influence of a temporary return to the wilderness—a dark version of the pastoral landscape—later echoed in Amiens's lyrical extension of the Duke's speech, whose comforting refrain seems to alienate the text of the stanzas:

> Blow, blow, thou winter wind,
> Thou art not so unkind
> As man's ingratitude.
> Thy tooth is not so keen,
> Because thou art not seen,
> Although thy breath be rude.
> Hey-ho, sing hey-ho, unto the green holly.
> Most friendship is feigning, most loving, mere folly.
> Then, hey-ho, the holly;
> This life is most jolly.
>
> Freeze, freeze, thou bitter sky,
> That dost not bite so nigh
> As benefits forgot.
> Though thou the waters warp,
> Thy sting is not so sharp
> As friend remembered not.
> Hey-ho! sing, &c. (2.7.175-94)

Shakespeare's forest of Arden is the best possible hide for those refugees, a natural wilderness—a 'desert place' for Orlando—where intruders may experience 'bare distress' in various forms (starvation, cold, animal attacks), which function as tests of 'civility.' The ordeals, whether physical or moral, through which all 'foresters' must go, are never beyond the compass of reason: even Orlando's 'distress' or 'folly' in love hardly has anything in common with Lear's revelation of 'bare distress' in madness:

Thou ow'st the worm no silk, the beast no hide, the sheep no wool, the cat no perfume. Ha! Here's three on's are sophisticated! Thou art the thing itself; unaccommodated man is no more but such a poor, bare, forked animal as thou art. Off, off, you lendings! Come, unbutton here. (*King Lear*, 3.4.105-12)

Nature never strips to nakedness in Arden, not even when Orlando checks the wound he has won from the lioness (4.3.147-49). On the contrary, *As You Like It* is a play where all the exiled characters wear disguises,

[*S.D.*] *Enter Duke Senior, Amiens, and other Lords dressed as outlaws* (*2.1*)

CELIA   I'll put myself in poor and mean attire, . . . (1.3.110)

ROSALIND   Were it not better . . .
That I did suit me all points like a man . . .? (1.3.113-15)

or dream of acquiring one:

JAQUES   I am ambitious for a motley coat. (2.7.43)

or regret their previous accoutrement:

ROSALIND   Alas the day, what shall I do with my doublet and hose! (3.2.211-12)

This obsession with dress and disguise and the threatening contamination of the inside by the outside is a recurrent dialectic in the play:

ROSALIND   Dost thou think, though I am caparisoned like a man, I have a doublet and hose in my disposition? (3.2.188-90)

It has been noted by critics as well as by Celia that, in appropriating a male dress, Rosalind-as-Ganymede also appropriates a male discourse on women: 'cucullus non facit monachum,' as the proverb has it; yet disguise for Rosalind-as-Ganymede, for Jaques-as-fool, for the Duke-as-outlaw, or for Oliver-as-wild man simultaneously has a transgressive and a liberating effect. This permeability of dress and body is echoed in Perdita's remark:

... Sure, this robe of mine
Does change my disposition. (*The Winter's Tale*, 4.4.135)

An analogous kind of permeability can be noted in the way Jaques and Orlando, like Duke Senior, 'translate' Arden back into the world of the polity:

'Sweep on, you fat and greasy *citizens*,
'Tis just the *fashion*. Wherefore do you look
Upon that *poor and broken bankrupt* there?'
Thus most invectively he pierceth through
The body of the country, city, court,
Yea, and of this our life, swearing that we
Are mere *usurpers*, *tyrants*, and what's worse,
To fright the animals, and to kill them up
In their *assigned* and native *dwelling-place*. (2.1.55-63, italics mine)

In literalizing Duke Senior's trope, Orlando inscribes himself in the long tradition of those amorous carvers:

O Rosalind, these trees shall be my books,
And in their barks my thoughts I'll character (3.2.5-6)

thus traducing what is most natural in man (passion) into a sign so highly coded by romantic culture as to become the object of a satirical rebuke on the part of Jaques (3.2.251-52).

In either case, Arden operates as both nurturing and specular, as it reflects each character's concerns and ethos. Orlando makes the forest the echo chamber of his passion as he wants to hang 'Tongues I'll hang on every tree, / That shall civil sayings show' (3.2.122-23), whereas Jaques's 'thousand similes' (2.1.45) reflect a set of values mostly concerned with the world of money and exchange which is reminiscent of Orlando's opening speech, itself explicitly concerned with economic matters:

... but poor a thousand *crowns*, ... report speaks *goldenly* of his *profit*.
... riders [are] *dearly hir'd*. But I, his brother, *gain nothing* under him but growth ... (1.1.2-13, italics mine)

Though the restraints of identity, gender, money and rank tend to dissolve in the forest, it cannot be argued that Arden is the place for an absolute purification from everything acquired, a total relinquinshing of nurture. As it is reasonably exacting, Arden is only relatively rewarding. In no way can it stand for an absolute like natural perfection, a notion difficult to justify in an Elizabethan context, as the concept of nature is eminently ambivalent: at the same time the model to imitate in art and the path to follow in pedagogy—hence a synonym for truth as opposed to artifice—, but also a symbol for the fall in the postlapsarian world. *A contrario*, if perfection there was in Arden, one might wonder why all the exiles should literally or metaphorically refer or even revert to the world of the Court. A temporary and relative harbour, Arden is the place of a possible process of education which tests the limits of 'civility,' but never excludes it:

> ... The thorny point
> Of bare distress hath ta'en from me the show
> Of smooth civility. (2.7.94-96)

Nature's powerful drives (power, hunger, or sex) are appetites which are explicitly dealt with in the play; it is through rituals and laws—*i.e.* culture—that they ought to be ruled, but the paradox is that, in the play, the farther one is from court, the further involved in poetry, wooing, ritual, and hyper-refined sentiment. In other words, nurture operates in Arden as a real protection against 'bare distress.' Though in a 'desert inaccessible,' Duke Senior elegantly appeals to Orlando's 'gentleness,' touching his vein at first:

> ... Your gentleness shall force
> More than your force move us to gentleness. (2.7.102-103)

'Gentleness' (103)—a quality ambivalently defined as either from birth, or acquired through good breeding—, 'Good manners' (92), 'civility' (93), are mere semantic variations on the key-word of the passage, *i.e. nurture* (97):

> ... Yet am I inland bred,
> And know some nurture. (2.7.96-97)

Orlando's intellectual appetite, verbalized in the opening scene, has its counterpart, physical hunger, dramatized here—a necessity that takes from him 'the show of smooth civility' (96).

The nature-nurture dialectic surfaces in those well-balanced, somewhat redundant, formulae whose equipoise is reached in Duke Senior's chiasmus:

gentleness . . . force
force . . . gentleness

Orlando's appetites thus undergo a disciplining under the tutoring supervision of two male figures, first a paternal one in the person of the Duke who immediately authenticates his patrilineal rights, then an ambiguous creature living in the 'purlieus of this forest' (4.3.77), a place itself characterized by its ambiguous legal and topographical definition:

1. A piece or tract of land on the fringe or border of a forest; originally, one that, after having been (wrongly, as was thought) included within the bounds of the forest, was disafforested by a new perambulation, but still remained in some respects, especially as to the hunting or filling of game, subject to provisions of the Forest Laws.
2. A place where one has the right to range at large; a place where one is free to come and go, or which one habitually frequents; a haunt; ones bounds, limits, beat.

The first two definitions in the *OED* give us hints of another imaginary space, equally liminal and reversible, the purlieus of desire, where fantasy offers such liberty to come and go, and where sexual definitions may vary in time. Ganymede's territory is thus a place in-between, where love therapy is possible through an act of faith:

I would cure you only if you would but call me Rosalind and come every day to my cot, and woo me. (3.2.405-406)

'Creeping like snail unwillingly to school,' Orlando undergoes an education about himself, about Rosalind and about the nature of love. First represented as a speechless combat ('Can I not say "thank you"?' 1.2.233, 'Thou art overthrown,' 1.2.244), then as ineloquent, self-absorbed love-poems where the mistress is inscribed within the lover's own discourse and appropriated in the form of the anatomic blazon, love then becomes a verbal game of dialogue and interplay. Orlando is not asked to use his pen but his wits, and to accept the relativity of time in order to become the 'true lover in the forest' (3.2.293). Just as he had 'thought that all things had been savage here' (2.7.107), he thinks that 'there's no clock in the forest' (3.2.291-92). This education begins by a series of denials ('there is *no* true lover,' 'By *no* means, sir,' 'there is *none* of my uncle's marks upon you,' 'I am sure you are *not* prisoner,' 3.2.293-354), until his own denial ('I can live *no longer* by thinking,' 5.2.48) announces that the 'idle talking' cure has reached a limit.

In Arden therefore the 'something that Nature gave [him]'— his gentility—has therefore been grafted, to use Rosalind's trope: 'I'll graft it with you, and then I shall graft it with a medlar' (3.2.113-6).

Nature and art thus seem to be reconciled, as Polixenes' conceit expresses it in *The Winter's Tale*:

> . . . we marry
> A gentler scion to the wildest stock,
> And make conceive a bark of baser kind
> By bud of nobler race. This is an art
> Which does mend nature—change it rather; but
> The art itself is nature. (4.3.92-97)

The nurturing process of Arden seems to develop beyond the chronological limits of the drama, as it had started in a pre-dramatic time; in another purlieus ('the skirts of this wild wood,' 5.4.154), another liminal experience of conversion from greed to renunciation takes place, and is followed in turn by another, as if this cycle was endless:

> JAQUES   To him will I. Out of these convertites
> There is much matter to be heard and learned. (5.4.179-80)

The perverted appetite of Jaques who 'can suck melancholy out of a song as a weasel sucks eggs' (2.5.11-12) has a corollary in his desire to cure the world. The black bile he gathers from the realm of art he wants to inject in the body politic in the form of a verbal purge, *i.e.* satire:

> Give me leave
> To speak my mind, and I will through and through

Cleanse the foul body of th'infected world,
If they will patiently receive my medicine. (2.7.58-61)

The clash between 'Signior Love' and 'Monsieur Melancholy'
can thus be viewed as the meeting of two forms of excess,
Jaques's experience as traveller and libertine being opposed to
Orlando's innocence and faithfulness. Paradoxically, the latter's
nurture seems to come from nowhere, and is acknowledged by
his brother and by Jaques as a gift of nature:

Yet he's gentle; never schooled, and yet learned; (1.1.155-56)

You have a nimble wit; I think 'twas made of Atalanta's heels. (3.2.267-
68)

His athletic fitness harmoniously balances his intellectual
abilities, and his capacity for love:

JAQUES   The worst fault you have is to be in love.
ORLANDO   'Tis a fault I will not change for your best virtue.
(3.2.273-74)

The natural wit he shoots at Jaques all along the scene contrasts
with what Jaques calls his 'humorous sadness' (4.1.18-19); this
melancholy, more than the effect of a 'humour' of nature, seems
to be a disposition bred by a certain kind of nurture, an excess of
experience, knowledge, or 'the sundry contemplation of [his]
travels' (4.1.17):

I fear you have sold your own lands to see other men's. (4.1.21-22)

—one more metaphor referring to the world of exchange which
might be construed in Faustian terms, 'lands' standing for 'soul'
or 'self.' 'Our mistress of the world' provides Jaques with the
knowledge and the experience on which his melancholy feeds.
He is outwitted by Orlando when the untutored youth holds up
a mirror to him:

ORLANDO   . . . Look but in, and you shall see him.
JAQUES   There I shall see mine own figure.
ORLANDO   Which I take to be either a fool or a cipher. (3.2.278-81)

The wit combat in which he defeats Jaques stages the allegorical victory of youth, health, and love over age, melancholy and experience. It is the third of Orlando's victories over male opponents, whether in the physical or in the symbolic mode. But if Orlando is 'physically mature and powerful,' he is 'socially infantilized and weak' (Montrose, 93).

At the outset of the play, his lament over the transmission of paternal heritage also expresses anxieties about the scarcity of nurture, both in the sense of nourishment and culture. *As You Like It* has indeed the highest frequency of occurrences of the term 'food' in the whole canon (twelve out of seventy) and the related terms ('dinner,' 'entertainment,' 'hunger,' 'chew'). Presented in the contrastive mode regularly at work in the play, it appears as aggression or kindness, predation or commensality, greed or generosity. In the former acceptation, it is a source of anxiety and potential conflict. From the initial stage of the play, it is expressed as the threat of wilderness at the heart of civilisation:

> Shall I keep your hogs, and eat husks with them? (1.1.35-36)

Orlando's irruption amidst the foresters with drawn sword projects on the wilderness an image of savagery that is immediately made incongruous by the Duke's gentle style which reconciles not only Orlando with his own followers, but also the notions of nourishment and gentility, and ultimately, that of fostering:

> ORLANDO   I almost die for food; and let me have it.
> DUKE SENIOR Sit down and feed, and welcome to our table.
> ORLANDO   Speak you so gently? Pardon me, I pray you.
> I thought that all things had been savage here,
> And therefore put I on the countenance
> Of stern commandment. (2.7.104-109)

Beneath the surface of disguise and environment, the scene is reminiscent of another symbolic meal among outlaws, the Cene, with Duke Senior as central, evangelical father-figure speaking in gnomic idiom (2.7.102-3), articulating another discourse of remembance. This nurturing encounter simultaneously re-establishes Orlando's broken connection with his own father through the warm expression of that love between the dead father and the exiled Duke, already mentioned in hyperbolic terms by Rosalind (1.2.218):

> DUKE SENIOR If that you were the good Sir Rowland's son,
> As you have whisper'd faithfully you were,
> And as mine eye doth his effigies witness
> Most truly limned and living in your face,
> Be truly welcome hither. I am the Duke
> That loved your father. (2.7.195-200)

Orlando's quest for Rosalind and love is not his priority when he decides to go to Arden and he 'does not go forward in pursuit of love until he has become friends with Duke Senior' (Erickson, 122). When he has met Rosalind-as-Ganymede, his duty to attend the duke at dinner prevails over his desire to go on conversing about love. The Duke's nurturant role thus simultaneously re-establishes a father-son relationship, confirms Orlando's identity through the recovery of patriarchal lineage, and 'takes over the prerogative of maternal nurturance' (Erickson, 124). The sweetness, comfort and gentleness of this male utopia is contrasted by threatening maternal symbols such as the lioness in suck which Orlando encounters and kills after he 'has retreated in the face of Rosalind's verbal aggressiveness. He has wandered through the forest "chewing the food of sweet and bitter fancy" (4.3.102), to seek the paternal figure who has nurtured him. Instead, he has found Oliver in a dangerously passive condition, threatened by a double source of oral aggression' (Montrose, 108). The scene highlights the reversibility of the process, since after he has saved his elder brother from the dangers of female predation, thus inverting the relationship of protective care between a younger and an elder brother, the reconciliation is once more expressed in terms of food:

> As how I came into that desert place—
> I' brief, he led me to the gentle Duke,
> Who gave me fresh array, and *entertainment*,
> Committing me unto my brother's *love*, (4.3.142-45)

In the same way as Orlando's victory over Charles the wrestler had effaced the image of the threatening 'mother earth' (1.2.184), the fostering, paternal image of the Duke effaces the gynophobic image of the threatening, maternal lioness. Simultaneously, another form of reversal occurs as fraternal 'kindness' triumphs over fratricidal strife, initiating a type of male relationship unmediated by woman. With Duke Senior as foster-father—foster is etymologically related to food—Orlando has proved to be faithful to the values of male heroism derived from his dead father. The Duke's paternal bond to Orlando is thus extended to Oliver after the latter's admission of brotherhood and before his encounter with Celia. In the Orlando-Rosalind connection likewise, the role of Rosalind as mediatrix between Orlando and her father follows the Duke's paternal bond to Orlando already established through his fostering care, itself the result of his former male friendship with Orlando's father, Rowland de Boys. Marital closure therefore only confirms and strengthens the male ties established by fostering: Orlando's father-in-law had previously appeared as foster-father.

Even before the—persistently anonymous—Duke appeared as a figure of seniority, remembrance and nurture, Adam had already appeared under the same three characteristics as foster-nurse to Orlando. His age is emphasized, and so is his fidelity to Sir Rowland's will before the motif of nurturance associated to love occurs. In the form of Adam's savings, 'the paternal inheritance blocked by Oliver is received indirectly from Adam' (Erickson, 123):

> ORLANDO   What, wouldst thou have me go and beg *my food*,
> Or with a base and boisterous sword enforce
> A thievish living on the common road?
> This I must do, or know not what to do.
> Yet this I will not do, do how I can.
> I rather will subject me to the malice
> Of a *diverted blood* and bloody brother.
> ADAM   But do not so. I have five hundred crowns,
> The thrifty hire I sav'd *under your father*,
> Which I did store to be *my foster-nurse*
> When service should in my old limbs lie lame,
> And unregarded age in corners thrown.

Take that, and *he* that doth the ravens *feed*,
Yea providently *caters* for the sparrow,
Be comfort to my age. Here is the *gold*.
All this I give you. (2.6.32-47 italics mine)

The correlation of gold, food, fatherly care ('he that doth the ravens feed') and inheritance ('diverted blood') is insistent enough to suggest that Adam's offer echoes and translates the initial crisis which merged the issues of legacy, education, blood, and food. Once in the forest, as in the case of Oliver, the relationship of fostering is inverted as Orlando assumes the fostering role:

> ADAM   Dear master, I can go no further. O, I die for food. Here lie I down and measure out my grave. Farewell, kind master.
> ORLANDO   Why, how now, Adam? No greater heart in thee? Live a little, comfort a little, cheer thyself a little. If this uncouth forest yield anything savage I will either be food for it or bring it for food to thee. (2.6.1-7)

The idea of the reversibility of nurturing clearly appears in Orlando's chiasmus ('food for . . . for food'), which expresses the threat inherent in the nurturing process later to be literalized in the lioness scene. Here, not only does Orlando exchange age roles in the manner of Aeneas and Anchises, but he also symbolically assumes the feminine identity of the doe:

> ORLANDO   Then but forbear your *food* a little while
> Whiles, like a doe, I go to find my faun
> And give it *food*. There is an old poor man
> Who after me hath many a weary step
> Limped in *pure love*; till he be first sufficed,
> Oppressed with two weak evils, age and hunger,
> I will not touch a bit. (2.7.127-33)

If Duke Frederick's greed is emblematic of one world and Duke Senior's generosity of another, there is room, at the skirts of the two worlds, for another form of transaction—that mediated by gold:

> CELIA   I pray you, one of you question yon man
> If he for gold will give us any food.
> I faint almost to death. (2.4.60-62)

In this context, Corin as shepherd and mediator appears as one more figure of male nurturance:

> ROSALIND   I prithee, shepherd, if that love or gold
> Can in this desert place buy entertainment,
> Bring us where we may rest ourselves and feed.
> Here's a young maid with travel much oppressed,
> And faints for succour. (2.4.70-74)

Celia's gold, like Adam's, stands for faithful love and acts as a visa to Arden as well as a protection against the dangers of the polity. On the fringe of the male enclave of Arden, gold operates transmutations of a pecular kind, converting the attributes of violence and power into those of sympathy and nurturance.

The transaction which spans the whole play, however, is that of legacy in the context of primogeniture, as argued by Louis Adrian Montrose in 'Social Process and Comic Form' (1981); there he defines primogeniture, referred to as 'the courtesy of nations' (1.1.43-44), not as a binding law, but as a flexible social custom, and establishes the connection between two apparently disparate aspects of transmission: 'Parents and children in Shakespeare's plays are recurrently giving or withholding, receiving or returning, property and love' (Montrose, 84). Shakespeare's departure from his source in this respect is significant. In Lodge's text, the dying father, Sir John of Bordeaux, priviledges Rosader, the youngest brother to the detriment of Saladyne:

> But unto Rosader, the youngest, I give my horse, my armor, and my lance, with sixteen plowlands, for if the inward thoughts be discovered by outward shadows, Rosader will exceed you all in bounty and honor. (Beecher, 98)

Saladyne's motivation is thus far more explicit and plausible than that of his Shakespearean counterpart, Oliver, who confesses that he does not know why he hates his younger brother. Joan Thirsk, in her article "Younger Sons in the Seventeenth century"[*] describes the implications of primogeniture as follows:

---

[*] Joan Thirsk, 'Younger Sons in the Seventeenth century,' *History*, London, 54, (1969), 358-77,

During the sixteenth century, to describe anyone as '*a younger son*' was a short-hand way of summing up a host of grievances. . . . *Younger son* meant an angry young man, bearing more than his share of injustice and resentment, deprived of means by his father and elder brother, often hanging around his elder brother's house as a servant, completely dependent on his grace and favour. (Thirsk, quoted by Montrose, 88)

Such grievances Orlando voices early in the play:

You have trained me like a peasant, obscuring and hiding from me all gentlemenlike qualities. The spirit of my father grows strong in me, and I will no longer endure it. (1.1.64-67)

until Oliver's about-turn after his conversion:

. . . my father's house and all the revenue that was old Sir Rowland's will I estate upon you, and here live and die a shepherd. (5.2.10-12)

Orlando's initial desire for recognition, which he later expressed as a refusal of Duke Frederick's heritage (1.3.217-18), is ironically echoed at the end of the play when he actually becomes Frederick's elder brother's heir, since Duke Senior, restored to his authority, restores the de Boys patrimony to Oliver, while the aspirations of the youngest brother as to property, power, and title are rewarded when the Duke acknowledges him as his own heir.

Thou offer'st fairly to thy brothers' wedding;
To one his lands withheld, and to the other
A land itself as large, a potent dukedom. (5.4.166-68)

Orlando's conversion from foster-son to son-in-law and heir, his recovery of patriarchal lineage, his fostering care for his elder brother and the restoration of Oliver are transformations that are all viewed as contrastive echoes to the various denials of fostering, such as Rosalind's banishment, Orlando's forced departure from home, or Oliver's forced quest for his brother.

Throughout this study, it has been argued that the play exemplifies the various implications of nurture—physical, symbolic and economic. Nurturing can thus be viewed as a complex process at work in Arden where the nurturing roles are taken on by men and where the symbols of female nurturance appear as threatening. This double inversion of conventional roles is inscribed in a general scheme of gender inversion.

Lastly, the desire for nurture appears as a priority from the very early stages of the play and echoes a motif insistent enough in the play—the subordination of the flesh to the spirit.

Pierre ISELIN

VI. 'Call me Ganymede' (1.3.124): The problem of identity and gender A review of criticism

> *The woman shall not weare that which pertaineth unto a man, neither shall a man put on a womans garment: for all that doe so, are abominations unto the Lord thy God.* (Deuteronomy 22, 5)

Clara Claiborne Park, "*As You Like It*: How can a Girl Be Smart and Still Popular," *The American Scholar*, 42, Spring 1973: 262-78, reprinted in *The Woman's Part*, pp. 100-16.

Contrary to what its title seems to suggest, this essay is not primarily concerned with Shakespeare's play. It is rather a wide-ranging exploration of feminine protagonists in literature, in the course of which Rosalind appears as 'more than witty.' *As You Like It* is her play. Rosalind is a political exile, but she shows no disposition to meddle in politics; it is not through her agency that her father is restored to his rightful place. Her wit is not, like Portia's, exercised in the service of sensible men engaged in the serious business of the world, nor are her jokes made at their expense. Her satire is, in fact, narrowly directed at two classes of beings—sighing lovers, and women. In the course of the fun, she works her way through most of the accusations already traditional in a large antifeminist literature (inconstancy, contrariness, jealousy, unfaithfulness, etc.) to the point where Celia tells her, 'We must have your doublet and hose pluck'd over your head, and show the world what the bird hath done to her own nest' (4.1.185-87).

Once Rosalind is disguised as a man, she can be as saucy and self-assertive as she likes. The characters, male and female, will accept her behaviour because it does not offend their sense of propriety; so will the audience, male and female, because they know she is playing a role. With male dress we feel secure. In its absence, feminine assertiveness is viewed with hostility. Male dress transforms what otherwise could be experienced as aggression into simple high spirits.

Nancy Hayles, "Sexual Disguise in *As You Like It* and *Twelfth Night*," *Shakespeare Survey* 32, 1979: 63-72.

Nancy Hayles deals with the three-tier complexity of the female page disguise in Renaissance drama, which Charles Lamb's remark on *Philaster* epitomises: 'What an odd double confusion it must have made, to see a boy play a woman playing a man: one cannot disentangle the perplexity without some violence to the imagination.' A central notion to Hayles' comparative approach to the two plays is that of control. 'The opening scenes of the play . . . draw a society where intimacy among women is implicitly contrasted with the rivalry among men. When the scene changes to the forest, several incidents seem designed as signals that the forest is a world where co-operation rather than competition prevails' (64). 'But soon we discover that competition is not altogether absent from Arden (Jaques *vs*. Duke Senior, Touchstone *vs*. William, Silvius *vs*. Ganymede). The situation is thus more complicated than a simple contrast between court competition and pastoral co-operation, or between female intimacy and male rivalry' (64). As the layers of Rosalind's disguise are added (Rosalind as Ganymede, then Ganymede as Orlando's Rosalind), the movement creates conflict; as they are removed, the movement 'fosters reconciliation.' 'When Rosalind-as-Ganymede insists that Orlando's Rosalind will have her own wit . . . Rosalind is claiming the right to be herself rather than to be Orlando's idealized version of her, as female reality is playfully set against male fantasy. In playing herself (which she can apparently do only if she first plays someone else) Rosalind is able to state her own needs in a way she could not if she were simply herself. Rosalind's three-fold disguise is therefore used to accentuate the disparity between the needs of the heroine and the expectations of the hero.' Her simpler disguise as Ganymede, which affects

Phoebe and Silvius, accentuates conflict as it 'inadvertently makes her Silvius's rival,' and 'causes Phebe's desires to be even more at variance with Silvius's hopes than before.' Phoebe and Silvius are caricatures of courtly love, and through them we are shown female manipulation and male idealization in a way that emphasizes the less pleasant side of the courtly love tradition.' 'Rosalind's self-indulgence in demanding Orlando's service without admitting anything in return could become a variation of the perversity that is anatomized for us in the relationship between Phebe and Silvius.' The layering of the disguise has served to accentuate the conflict between men and women; now the unlayering finally resolves that traditional tension between the needs of the female and the desires of the male (65).

The unlayering begins when Oliver appears to explain why Orlando is late—the tale has as its point that Orlando put the needs of his brother before his own natural desire for revenge. By overcoming the twin threats of female engulfment (the lioness in suck) and phallic invasion (the snake about to enter the sleeping man's mouth), 'Orlando conquers in symbolic form projections of both male and female fears.' Rosalind responds to Oliver's account by swooning. Her faint is a literal relinquishing of conscious control,' as well as an 'involuntary revelation of female gender.' Her swoon 'provides a feminine counterpart to Orlando's selflessness—his heroic and selfless act. Orlando's struggle and Rosalind's swoon mark a turning point.'

The play suggests that control is necessary to state the legitimate needs of the self, but also that it must eventually be relinquinshed to accomodate the needs of another. The workings of the disguise suggest that what appears to be a generous surrendering of self-interest can in fact bring consummation both to man and woman, so that rivalry can be transcended as co-operation brings fulfillment. Unexpected restoration, forgiveness, reconciliation, and conversion—all express the same paradox of consummation through renunciation that is realized in specifically sexual terms by the disguise.

The epilogue continues the paradox of consummation through renunciation that has governed sexual disguise within the play, as the final unlayering of the disguise coincides with a plea for the audience to consummate the play by applauding. For the last time, the unlayering of the disguise is linked with a reconciliation between the sexes as the boy actor speaking the epilogue appeals separately to the men and women in the audience.

Many problems considered in *As You Like It* (Duke Frederick's tyranny, Oliver's unfair treatment of Orlando, Phoebe's exultation over Silvius) stem from excessive control and the heroine exercises extraordinary control over the disguise. Within the play these two perspectives have been reconciled, and the joint applause of the men and women in the audience re-affirms that reconciliation and extends it to the audience (67). Because of the correspondence between Rosalind as controller of the disguise, and Shakespeare as controller of the disguised boy actor who plays Rosalind's part, Rosalind's control over her disguise is paradigmatic of the playwright's control over the play.

Robert Kimbrough, "Androgyny Seen Through Shakespeare's Disguise," *Shakespeare Quarterly*, 33 no. 1, Spring 1982: 17-33.

Robert Kimbrough first challenges the false assumption that Shakespeare and his colleagues readily exploited girl-into-boy disguise because their women were really men and their audiences knew it (17). To maintain that there has ever been a comic device based on the actual sex of the actors is to fly in the face of a generic essential casually remarked upon by Sidney and Johnson: 'people going to the theatre check their literal-mindedness at the door and willingly believe anything they are asked to believe; the theatre is where illusion becomes reality' (17). So we do Shakespeare a disservice not to accept his women as women (17).

Because a woman disguised as a man has both sexes in one, the theatrical device of girl-into-boy disguise within comedies offers a logical place to begin an analysis of Shakespeare's treatment of androgyny (19).

– Carolyn G. Heilbrun, *Toward a recognition of Androgyny* (1973): 'Androgyny seeks to liberate the individual from the confines of the appropriate.'

– June Singer, *Androgyny: Toward a New Theory of Sexuality* (1976): 'androgyny . . . in its broadest sense can be defined as the

One which contains the Two; namely, the male (*andro-*) and the female (*gyne-*). Androgyny is an *archetype* inherent in the human psyche. . . . [and] may be the oldest archetype of which we have any experience' (20).

– Cynthia Secor (Introduction to the 1974 issue of *Women's Studies*): 'Androgyny is the capacity of a single person of either sex to embody the full range of human character traits, despite cultural attempts to render some exclusively feminine and some exclusively masculine.'

Robert Kimbrough then contends that sex is genetically determined, whereas gender is not (19). Androgyny is, then, a striving for an ideal state of personal wholeness, a microscopic attempt to imitate a mythic macrocosm. Because life as experienced is fragmented, androgyny, of necessity, looks beyond duality back to a time when personhood experienced innate wholeness and unity, a time 'back there,' 'once-upon-a-time,' 'in the beginning'—or rather before the beginning (20).

There are seven examples of girl-into-boy disguise in Shakespeare: Julia, Portia, Nerissa, Jessica, Rosalind, Viola and Imogen (21).

In *As You Like It*, in order to suggest the androgynous dimensions of the characterization of Rosalind, Shakespeare provides within the play three special audiences for her playing: Celia, Orlando, and Phoebe.

In her first conversation with Celia, Rosalind keeps the attention on her first remark: the inequities and unfortunate lot of women.

Thus, when Rosalind is banished, it is almost with relief that she decides to put on an unnecessary but wished-for male disguise, behind which she can escape not just the court, but in part what has been so far her Fortune-dealt restricted feminine self (23).

Once in the forest, she consciously elects to stay in disguise: 'I will speak to him like a saucy lackey, and under the habit play the knave with him' (3.2.286-87).

What Rosalind's lines emphasize so far is 'the woman within the knave's clothes in order to maintain a sense of contrary doubleness' (2.4.3-4; 3.2.188-90; 3.2.238). Once she has spoken to Orlando, she mocks herself and mocks men by using her wit in the manner of men who belittle women's wit: 'Make the doors upon a woman's wit, and it will out at the casement; shut that, and 'twill out at the keyhole; shut that, 'twill fly with the smoke out at the chimney' (4.1.148-51). But alone with Celia, Rosalind can still be delightfully open and emotional: 'O coz, coz, coz, my pretty little coz, that thou didst know how many fathom deep I am in love! But it cannot be sounded. My affection hath an unknown bottom, like the Bay of Portugal' (4.1.190-91).

On the surface, then, Rosalind is now both male and female. To this duality, because she is not sure that either she or Orlando is ready for an open, mutual commitment, she adds the role of 'Rosalind,' which is a hidden way of being openly herself. As a man, she is freed from societal convention and can speak her *mind*. Also, because of her being a man, Orlando, relaxed in the presence of male company, can reveal his *emotions*. If Orlando knew he was in the presence of a woman, let alone Rosalind, he would once again become as tongue-tied as he had been at court (24).

Rosalind's gently chiding speech to Phoebe regarding her treatment of Silvius is so full of common sense that Phoebe would not tolerate it from another woman. When Rosalind receives Phoebe's letter, she is strategically and personally able to tease Silvius by toying with society's definitions of masculine and feminine because her own experience has taken her beyond the limitations of those definitions:

> ROSALIND   Why, 'tis a boisterous and a cruel style,
> A style for challengers. Why, she defies me,
> Like Turk to Christian. Women's gentle brain
> Could not drop forth such giant-rude invention,
> Such Ethiop words, blacker in their effect
> Than in their countenance. Will you hear the letter?
> SILVIUS   So please you, for I never heard it yet,
> Yet heard too much of Phoebe's cruelty. (4.3.32-39)

She has achieved a position as woman and man from which she can understand and mock the absurdity of the social restrictions caused by gender stereotyping; her seemingly anti-female jibes have not been understood as ways of wrestling with attributes created for women by society. Thus, by a directness allowed by an indirectness, Rosalind and Orlando find each other out. At the end, not only is Rosalind the magician she claims to be; she is herself the product of her magic (25). As a magician/alchemist, Rosalind will take the male-Rosalind and the female-Rosalind and merge them into a human-Rosalind:

> Believe then, if you please, that I can do strange things. I have since I was three years old conversed with a magician, most profound in his art, and not yet damnable. If you do love Rosalind so near the heart as your gesture cries it out, when your brother marries Aliena shall you marry her. I know into what straits of fortune she is driven, and it is not impossible to me, if it appear not inconvenient to you, to set her before your eyes tomorrow, human as she is, and without any danger. (5.2.56-65)

Through her interaction with both a man, Orlando, and a woman, Phoebe, Rosalind has been able to reach toward a fuller realization of her humanhood, or potential for androgyny (26). The power of sex in human intercourse has been present in the play through Audrey and Touchstone and, by report, Celia and Oliver, but the emphasis in the main plot has been on gender differentiations. In the epilogue Shakespeare brings sex and gender together in order to give a final plea on behalf of androgynous behaviour. Just as an actor's role is a disguise, so is gender a disguise, and all disguises must be removed for people to be themselves. Now, Rosalind the boy actor must push home that fact (27). 'If the Forest has been a magic circle for the characters in the play, so has the play been for the audience. . . . By stepping out of the play, as if out of the fiction, [Rosalind] exercises the genuine force of her magic by bringing us *into* the fictional. The play is our Arden.' Albert R. Cirillo ('Pastoralism Gone Awry,' p. 38).

Catherine Belsey, "Disrupting Sexual Difference: Meaning and Gender in the Comedies" (1985), reproduced in *Alternative Shakespeares*, vol. I.

Catherine Belsey establishes the connection between the construction of meaning, based on the Saussurean notion of difference, and that of gender. To disrupt the fixity of meaning, she argues, is to glimpse alternative possibilities. Likewise, the inevitable antithesis between masculine and feminine can be called into question by Shakespeare's comedy, in that it disrupts the system of differences, particularly sexual difference, and thus creates a plurality of signification, which unsettles the traditional polarity of meanings and 'the opposition defining the feminine as that which is not masculine' (178).

Barbara J. Bono, "Mixed Gender, Mixed Genre in Shakespeare's *As You Like It*," *Renaissance Genres: Essays on Theory, History, and Interpretation*, edited by Barbara Kiefer Lewalsky, 1986, reproduced in *Twentieth Century Interpretations of* As You Like It.

Barbara Bono seeks 'to erect a framework of contemporary feminist theory about a traditional genre-based analysis of the heroic, romantic, and pastoral strains in Shakespeare's *As You Like It*' (131), and to 'sketch both Orlando's and Rosalind's roles in the play on the basis of Chodorow's model for the formation of gender and identity' (134).

Like Coppélia Kahn,[1] Bono argues the applicability of Nancy Chodorow's theory of gender formation to the representation of male personality in Shakespeare's plays. Chodorow[2] revised Freud's classic accounts of masculinity and femininity, by stressing the temporal primacy of the mother and placing her as socializer: 'The male child defines himself in a tension-fraught opposition to his potentially engulfing mother, while the female child has the more complex and extended, if less extreme, task of simultaneously affirming a gender identity with the mother and an individual differentiation from her' (132). Kahn follows Louis Adrian Montrose's[3] sociological reading of the pastoral play. Focusing explicitly on the historically sensitive oedipal situation of

---

1.   Coppélia Kahn, "Excavating 'Those Dim Minoan Regions': Maternal Subtexts in Patriarchal Literature," *Diacritics*, 12 (1982), 37-41.
2.   Nancy Chodorow, *The Reproduction of Mothering: Psychoanalysis and the Sociology of Gender*, Berkeley and Los Angeles, 1978.
3.   Louis Adrian Montrose, "'The Place of a Brother' in *As You Like It*: Social Process and Comic Form," *Shakespeare Quarterly*, 32 (1981), 28-54.

brothers' rivalry over a paternal inheritance, Montrose dwells on the engaging plot of Orlando's rise that frames Rosalind's androgynous disguising. 'The "feminism" of Shakespearean comedy seems to me more ambivalent in tone and more ironic in form than such critics [those infatuated with Rosalind's exuberance] have wanted to believe' (Montrose, 53). Kahn's work suggests that from a male point of view both Rosalind and Arden are initially threatening but eventually beneficient manifestations of a nonfeminist maternal subtext. Bono argues that 'the patriarchal, oedipal crisis of the first act of the play is displaced back onto its preoedipal ground in the nature of the forest of Arden—that place named suggestively after Shakespeare's own mother, Mary Arden, and the forest near his birthplace at Stratford-on-Avon' (134). In the play, Arden appears as a sometimes harsh, sometimes nurturing 'Mother Nature.'

'Orlando's masculine heroic quest, couched simultaneously in the the language of biblical typology and classical epic, is resolved within Arden's "sweet style". There Rosalind, fully acting out romance's conventions of disguise, transforms the social perception of woman from the Petrarchan conventions that both idealize and degrade her to a new convention of companionate marriage. Unlike Orlando's simpler quest, Rosalind's "double-voiced" discourse, criticizing the subject of which she is a part, can thus offer a method for cultural change. She performs *within* the text the critical task feminists today must perform *toward the text as a whole*' (134).

Orlando, a victim of parricidal rage, experiences a potential regression to a threatening maternal subtext (Charles suggests how the young man may be 'desirous to lie with his mother earth,' 1.2.184), as his lack of good breeding and his fear of exile in an inhospitable nature (2.3.32-35) are expressed. Unlike Lear, Duke Senior exercises seemingly benign verbal control over his environment (2.1.5-17); the masculine governing identity has not been violently dislocated by exile. After the failure of the patriarchy in the first act, his 'sweet' stylization now permits the growth of Orlando's romantic art (137). Orlando, after initial conflict with paternal figures—his older brother and Duke Frederick—which nearly culminates in archetypal tragedy, experiences nature as harshly threatening. He is saved from its ravages by a kindly father figure who thus metaphorically restores the archetypal line of paternal descent. With the confidence of that masculine relatedness, he is able to play seriously at the civilized game of love without threatening his basic male heroic identity (138).

Meanwhile, similar social problems unfold differently in an aristocratic women's world. Rosalind's musings about the precarious social position of women in love (1.2.32-34) suggest that the Duke's exile, deeply felt though it is, is less important than her problematic femininity, especially without his protection (138). Exiled by her tyrannous uncle, Rosalind assumes masculine disguise as a safeguard against female vulnerability in a threatening male world. Though she seems to be on the verge of throwing off her masculine attire (3.2.211-12), as there is in theory no longer any need for it, she prefers to speak to Orlando in a 'double voiced' discourse that characterizes the relationship of female to male culture: 'I will speak to him like a saucy lackey, and under that habit play the knave with him' (3.2.286-87), *i.e.* she will defensively adopt the 'habit'—the clothing and habitual ways—of the dominant male culture, including its view of women (139). The Petrarchan tradition [see Part X, 'Petrarchanism']—which Shakespeare documents and criticizes in characters like Romeo, Orsino, or Troilus—imagines a chaste, inaccessible Dianalike woman as the object of the male speaker's love, engendering in him a narcissistically luxuriant range of contradictory emotions that further objectify her, retributively fragmenting her body [see Part X 'blazon'] (139). Within this self-generating fiction the only power women seem to have is the defensive one of refusal, for then, at least, they may put off being consumed and discarded (140). Rosalind observes the hitherto uncultivated Orlando's burgeoning conventional love poetry, and by remaining a boy, at first defensively distances herself from it (140). By retaining her disguise as a girlish boy, Rosalind simultaneously offers Orlando a chance to test 'the faith of [his] love' (3.2.406-407) within the relatively nonthreatening limits of supposed male discourse about women, and attempts to exorcise her own fears about committing herself to such a discourse (140). Having suffered an oedipal crisis in the first act of the play because of the exile of her father and the opposition of Duke Frederick, Rosalind too is thrown back upon nature. Unlike Orlando, however, she does not experience this preoedipal nature as harshly threatening; does she require the immediate assurance of a restored father figure? In Arden Rosalind discovers a female identity that will allow her to complete the difficult, triangulated resolution of a girl's typical oedipal crisis: differentiation from *and* continuity with the mother and transfer of affection from the father onto an appropriate heterosexual love object (141). In response to Ganymede's trying poses (3.2.387-403), Orlando remains constant and retains an essentially simple faith grounded in his newly secure identity in the Duke's service. Rosalind's action as Ganymede/Rosalind does not shock or shake his identity, in the way nature had earlier threatened to do.

Rosalind as Ganymede, however, transforms herself more thoroughly. As her words imply, she is not a dispassionate therapist: 'Love is merely a madness . . .' (3.2.381); her 'holiday humour' is as much used to exorcise her own fears as it is to criticize or educate her lover. In her interaction with Silvius and Phoebe, she becomes, quite to her surprise, the sexually ambiguous means—a boyish 'ripe sister' (4.3.88)—through which their hopelessly stalemated and conventional Petrarchan attitudes are softened toward reciprocal love (142). Rosalind-as-Ganymede's action within Silvius and Phoebe's play has a double relevance for her action within her own. It makes explicit her androgynous power, even while it implies her own subliminal desire to give herself to Orlando. It is necessary for her to misuse her sex, to soil her own nest, as Celia half-jokingly puts it (4.1.186-87), in order to hide the 'woman's fear' (1.3.118) in her heart.

With the picture of 'A wretched ragged man, o'ergrown with hair' (4.3.107) and menaced by a snake and a lioness, Arden has grown threatening again, recovered its maternal peril implied by the Ovidian 'suck'd and hungry lioness'—the masculine fear of return to nature emblematized as the supposed wild man (143). The threat presents itself to Orlando as a moral dilemma, for he recognizes the endangered man as his unnatural brother Oliver. In making 'kindness, nobler ever than revenge / And nature, stronger than his just occasion,' Orlando redeems Eden. The bloody napkin

Oliver brings to Ganymede/Rosalind emblematizes the male adversarial experience of the world of nature; it intrudes the reality of death into Arden. Because of it, 'Ganymede' promptly swoons and can hardly maintain her disguise.

In the final act of *As You Like It* Rosalind seemingly gives herself to the Duke her father so that he may give her to Orlando (5.4.19-20, 113-14). She thus reminds us that their initial attraction to each other was as much through their fathers—the old Sir Rowland de Boys whom Duke Senior loved as his soul (1.2.219)—as it was to their unmediated selves, and gives herself to the patriarchy toward which her defensive behaviour all along has been in reference (145).

In the metadramatic 'Epilogue,' for once, men bear the greater burden. the Elizabethan boy actor who played Rosalind conjures women to please themselves and men to play with women for mutual pleasure ('Epilogue,' 11-16). He thus inverts the sexological situation of the play itself, where Orlando had but to become assured in his male heroic identity, while Rosalind had had, through her disguise, her 'double-voiced' discourse, to accomodate herself to him. This final inversion in a consummately playful play suggests that men and women can work together—albeit often awkwardly—to transform a world not deterministically bound by its cultural conventions (147).

The question raised in the last section of Bono's reading of *As You Like It* is what kind of pastoral this play finally is. Despite its very firm grounding in contemporary social realities and the conventions of romantic and heroic discourse, the play remains conscious that its pastoral inside reflects a playful outside of continuing interpretation. Structured as a debate in all its details and its major patterns, *As You Like It* also invites us to enter its debates, ourselves 'busy actor[s] in their play' (3.4.55).

Phyllis Rackin, "Androgyny, Mimesis, and the Marriage of the Boy Heroine on the English Renaissance Stage," *PMLA*, vol. 102, no. 1, jan. 1987: 29-41.

Phyllis Rackin considers five Renaissance comedies which illustrate the changing conceptions of gender, androgyny, and theatrical mimesis—in particular as regards the representation of transvestite heroines. These plays are John Lyly's *Gallathea* (c.1587), Shakespeare's *Merchant of Venice* (c.1596), *As You Like It* (1599), and *Twelfth Night* (c.1601); and Jonson's *Epicoene* (1609). The study of this dramatic context is rewarding in that it correlates the theatre as a place of contention for competing ideologies—*e.g.* the changing conceptions of gender—, the attitude towards language at the dawn of the modern age, and the theory of theatrical mimesis at a time of open dispute. Though her point is barely substanciated, Rackin argues that the very figure of the androgyne was changing at the time of the Renaissance. The ambivalence of response evoked by the sexual ambiguity of the boy-heroine in masculine attire was further complicated by the ambivalent mythological tradition surrounding the figure of the androgyne, who could be 'an image of transcendence—of surpassing the bonds that limit the condition in a fallen world, of breaking through the constraints that material existence imposes on spiritual aspiration or the personal restrictions that define our roles in society. But the androgyne could also be an object of ridicule or an image of monstrous deformity, of social and physical abnormality. . . . Increasingly, the high Renaissance image of the androgyne as a symbol of prelapsarian or mystical perfection was replaced by the satirical portrait of the hermaphrodite, a medical monstrosity or social misfit, an image of perversion or abnormality' (29). The conception of the *super*natural androgyne thus seems to have given way to that of the *un*natural hermaphrodite, at a time when the imitation of nature became the standard by which art was to be judged.

The stance of Shakespeare in these three comedies is original in that, unlike Lyly and Jonson, 'he refuses to dissolve the difference between the sex of the boy-actor and that of the heroine he plays; and he uses his boy-heroine's sexual ambiguity not only to complicate his plots but also to resolve them' (31). 'On a stage where female characters were always played by male actors, feminine gender was inevitably a matter of costume, and in plays where the heroines dressed as boys, gender became doubly problematic, the unstable product of role-playing and costume' (29).

Stephen Greenblatt, "Fiction and Friction" in *Shakespearean Negotiations*, 1988.

Stephen Greenblatt reads stage transvestism and the fiction of sex change through the medical discourse of the Renaissance about sex change and gender, and draws on the context of the legal proceedings and literary testimonies.

Greenblatt considers cases of real or pretended hermaphroditism, and the medical discourse of the period, in particular the universal paradox of nature, *i.e.* 'on the one hand all bodies contain both male and female elements; on the other hand, there are not two radically different sexual structures but only one—outward and visible in the man, inverted and hidden in the woman.

In a remarkable study, *The Renaissance Notion of Woman*, Ian MacLean thus summarises the terms of the medical dispute that took place at the turn of the century between the late supporters of the one-sex theory, and those who opted for an appropriately differentiated physiology. One significant step of the latter school of thought was Gabriele Fallopio's [Fallopius] description of the female genitalia in his *Observationes anatomicae* (1561). Even though Descartes's anatomy still supported the Galenic alignment of genitalia, Galen's comparison of male and female genitalia (uterus=inverted penis, ovaries [*testes mulierum*]= testes) was rejected by the *neoterici*, and by the end of the century most anatomists had abandoned this parallelism. Maclean concludes that 'by 1600, in nearly all medical circles, . . . one sex is no longer thought to be an imperfect and incomplete version of the other' (33).

Greenblatt comes however to the conclusion that 'even when the belief that the woman was a defective male was abandoned by most physicians and the form of the female anatomy was attributed to function rather than inadequate heat, the notion of an alignment between the sexes proved surprisingly durable' (83), and considers that, though the medical discourses were far from being univocal, 'in the sixteenth and seventeenth centuries, physicians and laymen of sharply divergent schools agreed that male and female sexual organs were fully homologous' (79)— one must remember that the discovery of the ovaries only took place in the later seventeenth century and their specific functioning was not well understood until the nineteenth century. One consequence of this belief in differential homology is a fascination with the possibility of sex change—almost always from female to male, that is from defective to perfect. Among other prodigies of sex metamorphosis, Ambroise Paré, the celebrated French surgeon, recounts the story of Marie Germain, which Montaigne also cites in the First Book of his *Essays*:

> Passant à Vitry-le-François, je pus voir un homme que l'évêque de Soissons avait nommé Germain en confirmation, lequel tous les habitants de là ont connu et vu fille, jusques à l'âge de vingt-deux ans, nommée Marie. Il était à cette heure là fort barbu, et vieil, et point marié. Faisant, dit-il quelque effort en sautant, ses membres virils se produisirent; et est encore en usage, entre les filles de là, une chanson, par laquelle elles s'entravertissent de ne faire point de grandes enjambées, de peur de devenir garçons, comme Marie Germain. Ce n'est pas tant de merveille, que cette sorte d'accident se rencontre fréquent; car si l'imagination peut en telles choses, elle est si continuellement et si vigoureusement attachée à ce sujet, que, pour n'avoir si souvent à rechoir en même pensée et âpreté de désir, elle a meilleur compte d'incorporer, une fois pour toutes, cette virile partie aux filles.

The psychosomatic definition of gender which Montaigne gives here emphasises the transforming power of the sexual imagination, as Marie proves to be literally *What she will*. The case of hermaphroditism, which held such fascination for the Renaissance, thus raises the question of gender differentiation and determinate sexual identity in crucial terms. Two apparently contradictory theories of the origins of gender were provided by Jacques Duval, a French doctor who devoted particular attention to the study of hermaphrodites: a determinate sexual identity emerges
(1) when a double nature becomes single (when either male or female seed, copresent in every person, establishes dominance);
(2) when a single nature becomes double (when the unitary genital system divides into two distinct forms, internal and external, female and male.
'Identity is at once made possible and dissolved by the slippage between these conflicting theories: to this extent, though gender for the Renaissance has everything to do with determinate

boundaries (for the period was intolerant of ambiguity), it has equally to do with the friction between boundaries' (84-85). For Shakespeare, Greenblatt continues, 'friction is especially associated with verbal wit; indeed at moments the plays seem to imply that erotic friction *originates* in the wantonness of language and thus that the body itself is a tissue of metaphors or conversely, that language is perfectly embodied' (89), as can be exemplified in the exchange between Viola and Feste in *Twelfth Night* (3.1.1-10). The capacity of language to be inverted, turned inside-out, like a 'cheveril glove,' recalls the cases of sexual transformation. Gender confusion, which takes various forms in the play, is the theatrical version of the twinned sexual nature out of which gender identity emerges through adolescence.

Sexual indeterminacy may simply be seen as the dramatic projection onto the cross-dressed woman of the process of male individuation, a stage in this 'male trajectory of identity.' Transvestite theatre, with an all-male cast, thus represents the expected mode of gender representation in the 'teleologically male' representation of sex identity. One consequence of the homology between male and female sexes is 'an apparent homoeroticism in all sexuality' (92), hence the delicious confusions of *As You Like It,* which 'depend upon the mobility of desire' (93). But there is a further dimension to transvestism on the Elizabethan stage, as within or underneath the imaginary women's bodies, there are other bodies—those of the actors. Greenblatt concludes his study with a revelation about the theatrical cross-dressing: 'the open secret of identity—that within differentiated individuals is a single structure, identifiably male—is presented literally in the all-male cast' (93).

Jean Howard, "Crossdressing, The Theatre, and Gender Struggle in Early Modern England," *Shakespeare Quarterly*, vol. 39, no. 4, 1988: 418-40.

While Greenblatt asserts the single—'identifiably male'— structure of gender, and Belsey advocates a plural, non-binary reading of cross-dressing, arguing that the blurring of sexual difference opens possibilities of undoing the structures of nomination and domination based on strictly binary sexual oppositions, Jean Howard's important study questions both readings and documents the actual practice of wearing the clothes of the other sex, the steady attack of polemists and preachers, and the threat cross-dressing represented in a society based on hierarchy and subordination. The controversy that took place from 1580 onwards resulted in the dual publication of two polemical tracts, *Hic Mulier or the Man-Woman* and *Haec Vir*, which respectively attacked and defended cross-dressing, in particular that of the women of the City who were accused of transgressing both class and gender boundaries (420). Strong links appear at the period between a mannish woman and prostitution, female cross-dressing and the threat of female incontinence. The nature of the transgression was in fact double, sexual first but social too, since 'to transgress the codes governing dress was to disrupt an official view of the social order in which one's identity was largely determined by one's station or degree' (421). Dress transgression therefore did not signal social disruption, it constituted such disruption. For the Puritan polemist Philip Stubbes, clothes were 'given us as a signe distinctive to discern between the sexes, & therefore one to weare the Apparel of another sex, is to participate with the same, and to adulterate the veritie of his owne kinde' (*The Anatomie of Abuses*, 1583, C2v). The fixed system of correspondences between the outward appearance of dress (analogous to the signifier in the order of language) and the inward reality of sex (the referent) seems to echo a literal attitude towards language as a closed system of representation. While limiting the scope of Greenblatt's medical sources, and their implication that only male genitalia were to be seen in both sexes, Howard finds support of a two-sex gender system not only in the Bible, but also in the writings of the Puritan polemists. Antitheatrical tracts definitely use the language of separateness, not of continuity, in gender matters. But the reading of cross-dressing is different whether it is a man—or a boy—who theatricalises the self as female, or a woman who wears male attire. The former case is shameful, and 'invites playing the female's part in sexual congress' (424), whereas the latter implied sexual incontinence, excessive appetite, rather than sexual perversion. 'In a period of social dislocation in which the sex-gender system was one of the major sites of anxiety and change, female cross-dressing in any context had the *potential* to raise fears about women wearing the breeches and undermining the hierarchical social order' (428). The charivari was then the communal ritual through which these unruly women were disciplined. As for the role of the theatre in gender definition, it may thus be envisaged either as the transformation of the transgression into a fiction that depoliticised it, or as agent of cultural transformation.

Valerie Traub's *Desire and Anxiety* (1992) offers a reading of *Twelfth Night* and *As You Like It* in a chapter entitled 'The homoerotics of Shakespearean comedy.' There she departs from the psychoanalytic and early feminist readings of the transvestism of *As You Like It* and *Twelfth Night* which 'stress the liberating effect caused by the temporary inversion of hierarchical gender arrangements, "through release to clarification," to use C. L. Barber's influential phrase' (119). Valerie Traub questions whether gender anxiety is the salient factor of homoerotic desire, anxiety and desire being the two sides of the same erotic coin (121). 'By means of her male improvisation, Rosalind leads the play into a mode of desire neither heterosexual nor homoerotic, but both heterosexual *and* homoerotic' (124). What attracts Phoebe to Ganymede are precisely those qualities that could be termed feminine (3.5.110-20). Is there not a sense in which Rosalind/Ganymede *elicits* Phoebe's desire, constructing it even as she refuses it (126)? Indeed, as a male, her sense of power is so complete that s/he presumes to tell Silvius to tell Phoebe, 'that if she love *me*, I charge her to love *thee*' (4.3.72).

'Homoerotic desire in *As You Like It* thus circulates from Phebe's desire for the feminine' in Rosalind/Ganymede to Rosalind/Ganymede's desire to be the 'masculine' object of Phoebe's desire (126). Orlando's 'courtship' of Ganymede 'requires less his willing suspension of disbelief than the ability to hold in suspension a dual sexuality that feels no compulsion to make arbitrary distinctions between kinds of objects' (127).

As a 'ganymede,' Rosalind would be expected to play the part of of a younger, more receptive partner in an erotic exchange. S/he thus not only inverts gender roles; s/he disrupts alleged homoerotic roles as well (127). 'The play does not end with Hymen's bars and bands, but with a renewed attack on the pretensions of erotic certitude. In a repetition of her previous gender, and erotic mobility, Rosalind-cum boy actor, still wearing female attire, leaps the frame of the play in order to address the audience in a distinctly erotic manner (Epilogue 16-19)' (128).

One may also find analyses related to gender in essays less precisely centered on *As You Like It*, as for instance:

Alan Bray, "Homosexuality and the Signs of Male friendship in Elizabethan England," *History Workshop*, 29, Spring 1990: 1-19.

Tracey Sedinger, "'If Sight and shape be true': The Epistemology of Crossdressing on the London stage," *Shakespeare Quarterly*, vol. 48, Spring 1997, no. 1: 63-79.

Pierre ISELIN

VII. *As You Like It:* 2.4
A Textual Commentary

Rosalind, Touchstone and Celia, after being exiled from court, arrive in the forest of Arden in a state of physical and moral exhaustion ('weary'). The scene prepares the spectator for Orlando's unmannerly intrusion amidst the group of Duke Senior's foresters, when he violently requests food for the old servant Adam whom he will later carry in his arms on stage (2.7). Shakespeare stresses the idea that liberty is less given than acquired, that it is the result of deprivation and pain (see Duke Senior's Stoic stance in 2.1.5-17) rather than a simple matter of breathing a different air. Shakespeare's green world does not exactly coincide with the idyllic pastoralism of Sidney, Lyly or Lodge. It is a wintry, barren place where one must walk and bear one's cross, an occasion for Shakespeare to remind us that material and physical hardships do exist in Arden.

Still, an interference between the world of the court and that of the traditional pastoral is achieved in the little play within, or show, which is offered in the conversation between two shepherds, Corin and Silvius, overheard by the three court exiles. Silvius is the archetypal Petrarchan lover and the literary shepherd *par excellence.* His love complaint will create some sentimental feedback in Rosalind (ll. 41-42) and a number of chain reactions, of echoes and commentaries that will further feed the plot of this comedy, since, as Rosalind exclaims, 'the sight of lovers feedeth those in love' (3.4.52). In this set of Chinese boxes, frame play and inner play interlock, as the spectators and actors of the comedy mutually influence one another, just as the wrestling scene watched by Rosalind and Celia had led to the victory of Orlando over Charles but also to the champion's being overthrown by love (1.2.244). In a similar way, the hunters become the hunted, 'pierced through' by the shafts of Jaques's satire. In both cases, everything boils down to a question of point of view, of discourse or of commentary. Here, the problem is no longer a question of manners or of life style as in 2.1 but of 'pangs of unrequited love,' of 'midnight pillows' and youthful 'folly.'

I. The pageant of pastoral love

Pastoral in *As You Like It* is first and foremost posture. It is here embodied by the shepherd youth Silvius, whose name is a byword for the forest (from the Latin 'silva'). Like the wounded deer, another 'native burgher of this desert city' (2.1.23), he weeps because of human cruelty. It is not men however who make him suffer, but a woman, Phoebe, who has shot him through with her love arrows. Love and hunting are indeed reversible worlds in the play, as the subsequent exchange between Celia and Rosalind reveals:

> CELIA   . . . I found him [Orlando] under a tree,
> like a dropped acorn— . . . There lay he,
> like a wounded knight— . . . He was
> furnished like a hunter—
> ROSALIND   O ominous—he comes to kill my heart. (3.2.226-38)

Besides sighing on 'a midnight pillow' (l. 24), love is associated with folly (l. 31), with 'actions most ridiculous' (l. 27) and with a melancholy cult of solitude ('broke from company / Abruptly,' ll. 37-38). Silvius's speech, like Touchstone's, is a long chain of conditions linked by a series of 'ifs' (there are four occurrences of the word in twelve lines). These allow the alternate expression of doubting, questioning and challenging. At the same time, it is a poetic posture, as can be seen by its highly formal enunciation. The shepherd's love ejaculations are arranged into the intricate pattern of a 'love sonnet' or 'dizain,' the restricted form cultivated by Maurice Scève in his *Délie*, here using the Sapphic verse, *i.e.* two pentameters followed by a line of four syllables used as a burden 'Thou hast not loved.' In Silvius's eclogue, love is defined by a string of negative comparisons, through of series of exclusive or suspensive conditions, 'If thou hast not . . . thou hast not loved.' We thus learn what love is not, rather than what love exactly consists of. Furthermore, the name of the beloved is repeated three times, like an incantation ('O Phoebe, Phoebe, Phoebe') that anticipates on Jaques's 'Ducdame, ducdame, ducdame' (2.5.50), a formula which he explains as 'a Greek invocation to call fools in a circle' (2.5.55). Thus, love appears as a show, but also as an occasion for verbal or magic incantations. It is here the counterpart of the traditional pastoral eclogue, the poetic contests in which the shepherds of classical or Renaissance Arcadia are generally involved.

Poles apart from the bashful pastoral lover, Touchstone appears as someone whose very trade precisely consists in never forgetting that he has a body, a pair of legs, a stomach and sexual organs. He ignores all sexless plants and invertebrate animals like the snail or the snake used by Rosalind-Ganymede (4.1.47 and 4.3.71) as comic analogies or 'objective correlatives' to mock the tardiness or passiveness of the male lover.

II. The physical and financial realities of the forest

a. Body and bawdy

Touchstone's way is his playful literal-mindedness. He begins by substituting 'legs' to Celia's 'spirits' and by using the verb 'to bear' transitively to mock Celia's intransitive 'bear with.' This, in turn, will be beautifully denied by the sight of Orlando bearing old Adam in his arms despite his own physical exhaustion. On the other hand, Touchstone, like Feste in *Twelfth Night*, is always looking for some kind of financial reward for his jesting as he cynically refuses any gratuitous action when he exclaims 'I should bear no cross if I did bear you, for I think you have no money in your purse' (ll. 11-12). In fact he is wrong, here as Celia said, just before leaving for Arden, 'Let's away / And get our jewels and our wealth together,' 1.3.132-33), which will allow her and Rosalind to buy Corin's farm and hence to find a home during their time of stay in the forest. Shakespeare slyly suggests that all the pastoral conversions or miracles cannot bypass the most elementary economic realities.

The first way of re-establishing reality is by calling attention to the sphere of material life through Touchstone's verbal clowning when he gives a prosaic and parodic echo to Silvius love lamentations (ll. 43-52). He substitutes Jane Smile, the

pretty milkmaid with an evocative name, for the cruel
shepherdess Phoebe. He too refers to nocturnal emissions
('coming a-night to Jane Smile,' l. 45) but, in this case, he does
not seem to refer to simple 'sighing'! He says that he 'broke [his]
sword upon a stone,' a sexual double-entendre suggesting self-
abuse or premature ejaculation like Celia's mockery of the
sexually immature Orlando who 'breaks his staff, like a noble
goose' (3.4.40). The erotic thus ruins the heroic as it turns it
upside down. This also means that he broke his 'word' given the
current reversibility of 'sword' and 'words' in the topsy-
turvydom of professional nonsense or foolery. Thus, in his
wooing of Jane Smile, the clown simultaneously confesses that he
broke his word and stupidly loosed or lost his semen... On top of
that, there is the misundertanding about the mistaking of one
object for another, a confusion that can be described as a form of
fetishism, when Touchstone fondly remembers the 'kissing of her
batlet... of her cow's dugs' or the 'wooing of a peascod instead of
her.' The word 'peascod' can also be reversed into 'codpiece,'
which evokes the homoerotic substitutes in a comedy where
Ganymede will be playing the part of 'Rosalind' for Orlando.
Language toys here with androgyny in truly Marlovian fashion.
Words and costume are the vehicles of a protean desire marked
by its mutability, its instability, by a series of cross-purposes, by
cross-dressing and criss-crossing. Touchstone uses chiasmus and
symmetrical repetitions to underline this when he says 'as all is
mortal in **nature**, so is all **nature** in love *mortal* in folly.' If Silvius
embodies a form of obsessional fixation of desire, Touchstone
stresses its unstable and protean nature, its disguises and its
willingness to be exchanged against a variety of other objects.

When he says that 'We that are true lovers run into strange
capers' (ll. 50-51), the word 'caper' evokes the goat through its
Latin etymology, while it also refers to the associated ideas of
caprice, Ovid and metamorphosis. Touchstone is the poet of
capricious love, whose forms and objects are always changing,
and he will indeed later refer to his model, 'the capricious poet
honest Ovid' (3.3.6). He takes his stance as woodland satyr
(quite different in tone from Jaques, the libertine turned
satirist), as polymorphous pervert grounding his philosophy on a
pagan, Ovidian theology of libertinism.

b. Money

If the forest is no disembodied world, it is not a world where money is unheard of. Charles, the Duke's wrestler, had mentioned 'the golden world' in 1.1.113, without realizing that the Golden Age he was referring to was a travellers' Eldorado or, at least, a place where people know good money from bad, true from counterfeit and where gold remains necessary for a number of financial transactions mentioned by Corin (ll. 79-99).

Celia had already alluded to the possibility of buying food from the shepherd ('If he for gold will give us any food,' l. 61) while Rosalind will settle for the farm, the sheep and the shepherd ('Buy thou the cottage, the pasture, and the flock / And thou shalt have to pay for it of us,' ll. 91-92).

Indeed, old Corin is marked by lack of food and general penury: 'By reason of his absence there is *nothing* / that you will feed on.' The laws of hospitality have become obsolete, the shepherd is deprived of the revenues of his work and he owns nothing at all. Behind the pastoral disguise, economic realities are looming large. The conditions of employment are getting worse and worse thus affecting the rural economy:

> I am shepherd to another man
> And I do not shear the fleeces that I graze. (ll. 77-78)

It is significant that sheep are here referred to through a metonymy ('fleeces') that stands for their financial value. In other words, sheep are replaced by fleeces to be sold for wool. Furthermore, there may well be here a contamination of meanings between the verbs 'to shear' and 'to share,' thus reinforcing the idea that the owner is no sharer. Even in the pastoral world, the law of a market economy depending on profit is what seems to matter most. Corin sighs when confronted with this ungrateful and 'churlish' master (l. 79), just as Silvius will when he thinks of his proud, inaccessible mistress. Every man must bear his cross. If the master is absent, the mistress is distant, and there seem to be few reasons to rejoice in Arden...

III. Desire, memory and exchange

This scene successively and successfully dramatizes the transactions of desire and trade in an environment normally devoted to the projection of idealized views of life. A note of subtle irony thus tinges the pageant of grief and lament expressing the fact that both shepherds, young and old, are in deadends. It is the 'miracle' of Rosalind-Ganymede's arrival in Arden that will provide a way out for Corin just as her intrusion in the affairs of Silvius and Phoebe will undo the love block and lead to their marriage at the end. Her therapy consists in re-establishing the circulation of money and desire in the paralyzed pastoral sphere.

a. Desire and memory

The lover here appears as the fastidious accountant of his sighs and sleepless nights. It is ironical though that the older shepherd, Corin, has forgotten every item of this obsessional list ('a thousand that I have forgotten,' he says to the bemused Silvius, l. 29). But the sight of his sorrowful plight re-opens Rosalind's wound as she is led to recollecting her own love memories. Touchstone then quickly blows away the instant of sentimentality by giving a parodic echo of the scene as he embarks in a series of prose variations on his own love memories, all opening with the same ritual formula 'I remember' which he repeats three times. This echoes Orlando's initial 'I remember' (1.1.1), another dialogue between a young and an old man (Adam) serving as a prelude to the exchanges between Silvius and Corin.

b. Exchanges

But Touchstone's remembrance is a comic re-membering which puts together the grotesque or monstrous body of the milkmaid's batlet, the cow's dugs and a peascod! It serves as a warning against the wanderings of love leading to blindness, ridicule or suffering. It foreshadows Orlando's wooing of a young man, Ganymede, in the name and place of his Rosalind. Finally, it shows how easily desire may trade its object against a variety of substitutes, just like gold which stands for what it has the power to buy:

> . . . If that love *or* gold
> Can in this desert place buy entertainment. (ll. 70-71)

The sheep are not grazed here as in standard pastoral drama, they stand for merchandise, for the value of their fleeces. As in *The Merchant of Venice*, where in a sinister echo to Gratiano's triumphant exclamation 'We are the Jasons, we have won the fleece,' Salerio, referring to the commercial losses of Antonio, answers 'I would you had won the fleece that he has lost,' thus adding a bitter pun on the word 'fleets' (3.2.240-41). Similarly, in *As You Like It*, Corin's 'fleece' is an ironical answer to Charles' early claim that the forest of Arden is a golden world where 'many young gentlemen *fleet* the time carelessly' (1.1.111-12). The pun here is all the more likely as Shakespeare indirectly assimilates the gentlemen to sheep when he writes that they '*flock* to him [Duke Senior] every day . . .'

All the same, Corin agrees to be Celia's substitute and to buy his master's estate in her name:

> Assuredly the thing is to be sold.
> Go with me. If you like upon report
> The soil, the profit, and this kind of life,
> I will your very faithful feeder be,
> And buy it with your gold right suddenly. (ll. 95-99)

So, just as Corin buys the estate in the name of Celia, Orlando will woo Ganymede in the name of Rosalind. The forest's Saturnalia work through a series of masks and namesakes as they invest a number of changelings who will deal with the handy dandy of desire and trade. Master and servant, slave and mistress, owner and namesake all exchange roles as the transactions of love and commerce are being carried out under the cloak (or skirt?) of the forest and of the pastoral world.

Shakespeare's pastoral does not upset or abolish the social hierarchy, it is content with a temporary suspension (what Jaques calls an 'intermission,' 2.7.32) of its rules and decorum, like carnival which allows for a free but short-lived mixing of social and sexual orders to operate as a safety valve. In *As You*

Like It, the safety valve is essentially a verbal one, since the main transgressions in the play belong to the sphere of discourse. In order to cope with the incantatory, obsessional language of the lover, the fool's witticisms or *jeux d'esprit* introduce a number of modulations as well as a certain relaxation in the world of speech. Cross-dressing and verbal antics serve to restore the possibilities of exchange in a paralyzed society which fails to get around the nothingness of desire (Phoebe who feeds on Silvius's love without giving back anything) or the nothingness of money (Corin's churlish master who hoards his gold and does not care for 'hospitality').

The main lesson taught in Arden is that one has to give in order to receive. Shakespeare's festive comedy is based on an economy of the gift and on the virtues of exchange, a joyful way of subverting the danger of selfish or predatory habits. Flirtatiousness and avarice are here placed on the same level, as the coy shepherdess and churlish master are placed back to back. For the worlds of desire and trade, it is good to know how to open or unbind your purse as it is the only way one can find 'Infinite riches in a little room' (a line echoed from Marlowe's *Jew of Malta* in 3.3.11-12).

François LAROQUE

VIII. Commentaire III.3

1. Situation

Cette scène se situe au début de ce que l'on peut appeler la deuxième partie de la pièce, celle consacrée à l'amour et à la réconciliation. L'hiver de l'exil et de la haine voit sa dernière illustration dans la très brève première scène de l'acte 3 où le duc Frédéric confisque les biens d'Oliver qu'il somme de ramener Orlando mort ou vif. Ganymède et Aliena, c'est-à-dire Rosalind et Célia sous leur déguisement respectif, rencontrent Orlando dans la forêt d'Arden où il affiche son amour pour Rosalind dans les poèmes qu'il placarde sur les arbres. Le pacte est alors conclu, il accepte de traiter Ganymède comme s'il s'agissait de Rosalind. La scène 3 de l'acte 3 nous présente la contagion de l'amour dans une nature qui prépare le printemps célébré deux actes plus tard (5.3) par la chanson des pages dont le refrain rappelle « Sweet lovers love the spring ». L'amour, qui comme de juste occupe d'abord et avant tout les protagonistes, trouve sa réplique thématique et son contrepoint stylistique à un niveau social inférieur dans l'association amoureuse du bouffon Touchstone avec la gardeuse de chèvres Audrey, personnage qui fait son apparition dans III. 3. Nous la reverrons en scène à trois reprises par la suite mais elle y sera très peu loquace ou silencieuse.

2. Structure

La scène se compose de deux épisodes articulés autour de l'arrivée du prêtre Sir Oliver Martext (57). Le premier volet présente la cour faite, à sa façon, par Touchstone à Audrey et son acceptation par cette dernière dans le style qui lui est propre. Jaques en retrait écoute l'échange et commente. Le deuxième volet est marqué par l'intervention ouverte de Jaques qui fait renoncer Touchstone à un mariage à la sauvette. Le mouvement général de cette scène de parodie amoureuse rustique — vulgaire, par contraste avec la parodie courtoise rustique offerte par Silvius et Phébé — conduit donc un sursis du projet matrimonial de Touchstone et à une déception qu'Audrey exprimera en revenant en scène (5.1.3-4). Dans l'économie générale de la comédie cet ajournement, aussi surprenant en soi que le projet nuptial lui-même, permet le regroupement final de tous les mariages dans la scène finale qui, à cet égard, bat un record du drame shakespearien puisqu'elle en présente quatre selon une palette socialement variée, allant du sommet de la hiérarchie aristocratique à l'échelon le plus modeste de la vie rustique.

3. L'acteur et la marge : Jaques

Dans les livres anciens, la marge bien souvent n'est pas blanche mais remplie à point nommé de gloses, de déclarations gnomiques, de mises en exergue, de citations d'œuvres sources ou d'analogues, bref elle guide l'attention du lecteur, conduit son œil aux points décisifs de la chronique, souligne les temps forts d'une histoire dramatique, les met en perspective. Elle relève d'une culture essentiellement axée sur l'analogie mais, qui, pour cette raison même, saisit la différence plus volontiers dans son état d'inversion terme pour terme de la norme que sous forme d'écarts plus discrets. On trouve au théâtre une stratégie déictique voisine de celle pratiquée par l'imprimé où le dramaturge trouve la source des histoires qu'il met en scène. Le Chœur dans *Henry V*, et ici Jaques sont des personnages marginaux dans ce sens rhétoriquement fort que nous venons de définir. Jaques trouve sa scène à lui dans la marge. C'est là qu'il prospère comme témoin et commentateur de l'existence et de ses jeux qu'il saisit au cœur de ce qui est la scène des autres. C'est vrai de la chasse avec sa cruauté et les dégâts qu'elle occasionne dans le monde vert, seul recours contre la tyrannie de la cour, mais pourtant transformé en tyrannie contre les animaux qui l'occupent *ab origine*. C'est vrai de l'autre chasse, amoureuse celle-ci, qui se développe dans la forêt d'Arden quand la dynamique de la comédie opère la nécessaire transition de l'hiver de l'oppression au printemps de sa résolution sentimentale heureuse. En retrait du couple qui occupe le devant de la scène, Jaques, par ses apartés au long du premier épisode, filtre et colore la vision du spectateur, dans la tradition des scènes d'espionnage qu'affectionnent, de manière égale à la Renaissance en Angleterre, veine comique et veine tragique. Les trois apartés (7-8 ; 28 ; 41) sont suscités par le discours de Touchstone qui semble retenir seul l'attention de Jaques. D'abord par une prétention dérisoire à la culture — allusion à Ovide par laquelle Touchstone entend briller à peu de frais aux yeux d'Audrey — que l'aristocrate Jaques dénonce dans une figure de comparaison marquée par le bathos : « O knowledge ill-inhabited; worse than Jove in a thatched house » (7-8). L'allusion savante à la visite de Jupiter et de Mercure dans la chaumine de Baucis et Philémon établit, elle, la maîtrise du sujet par Jaques. La dérision de l'inférieur est une des formes possibles de la satisfaction de soi. Le deuxième aparté commente au contraire une métaphore diététique d'un style très quotidien : « honesty coupled to beauty is to have honey a sauce to sugar » observe Touchstone à l'adresse d'Audrey. « A material fool », commente Jaques en jouant sur les deux sens de l'adjectif : « substantiel/chargé de sens » et « bassement matériel ». Le sarcasme de Jaques, systématique, procède en tenaille. Il attaque l'adversaire dans la partie haute et dans la partie basse du spectre, ne lui laissant que peu de chance de s'en tirer. Ce deuxième aparté qui désigne le bouffon dans son état rappelle la fascination que Jaques éprouve pour ce métier de dérision exercé en toute immunité parce que sous la protection de l'autorité la plus haute. On se souvient avec quelle énergie le Duc exilé a refusé à Jaques (2.7.62-9) la licence de fol qu'il lui demandait dans sa Cour d'exilés. Attaqué par Jaques, Touchstone reste celui qui occupe l'attention de l'homme dont l'excès humoral voudrait, pour mieux s'épancher, l'excuse de la marotte. Le dernier aparté (41) vise seulement à accentuer l'expectative du spectateur qui vient d'apprendre l'imminence de la rencontre entre Touchstone et le prêtre qui doit officier. Le spectateur du théâtre trouve en Jaques son relais sur scène.

　　Dans le deuxième épisode où Jaques révèle sa présence et offre de conduire la mariée à l'autel, il quitte — et c'est une

exception dans la pièce — son rôle marginal pour infléchir
l'action dramatique comme elle doit l'être puisqu'il est interdit
de représenter en scène les cérémonies de la liturgie chrétienne.
Présentée par lui-même comme un geste moral (« Get you to
church, and have a good priest that can tell you what marriage
is », 76-78), l'intervention de Jaques obéit essentiellement à une
nécessité dramatique et ce serait une erreur de voir le
personnage révéler à cet instant une profondeur morale sans
rapport avec la vie de débauche que lui a prêtée le Duc exilé
(2.7.65-69). Loin de nous trouver devant une solution de
continuité dans la peinture morale du personnage, ce dernier
illustre une continuité fonctionnelle : qu'il s'agisse de chasse ou
de mariage, Jaques est, quand il le peut parce qu'ayant prise sur
l'événement, un empêcheur de tourner en rond ce qui est bien,
en partie, la vocation du fol auquel il s'identifie.

4. Jeux de mots, parodie : Audrey, Touchstone, Sir Oliver Martext

Déjà introduit par Corin et Silvius (2.4), le monde de la
pastorale perd de son idéalité avec Audrey et ses chèvres. Elle
représente l'état de nature ou presque, une sensualité simple
mais non dénuée de quelque idée morale. Elle veut Touchstone
mais se défie du langage dont il la crible : « I do not know what
poetical is ». Une fois établi le lien entre poésie et fausseté (16-
17), elle revendique son honnêteté par une litote catégorique
ainsi que l'aspect repoussant qui de son point de vue, et
certainement dans son cas particulier, va de pair avec
l'honnêteté : « I am not a slut, though I thank the gods I am
foul ». Le sens de « foul » dépend totalement de choix fait pour
le théâtre : distribution du rôle, choix de costume et de
maquillage, gestuelle. Sur la scène moderne une actrice jolie et
seulement mal fagotée fera de « foul » une exagération et une
naïveté charmantes, une peau noircie de crasse et de boue, des
cheveux emmêlés et graisseux, un sourire brèche-dent
donneront son sens plein au mot. Si un geste obscène vient
appuyer « foul », c'est la litote « I am not a slut » qui prendra
soudain valeur d'antiphrase. Le degré de redondance des signes
visuels et verbaux règle non seulement la représentation

d'Audrey comme sujet, mais comme elle est objet de désir, cela engage évidemment la réception du personnage de Touchstone. C'est ce dernier qui domine toute la scène par la prolixité à laquelle l'engage ou le condamne sa fonction de bouffon. Jeu de mots, jeux d'esprit et cynisme le définissent. Ce dernier trait est révélé à la fois dans les échanges avec Audrey (*Audrey*. « Would you not have me honest? » *Touchstone*. « No, truly . . . », 24-25), et dans ceux avec Jaques (*Touchstone*. « I am not in the mind but I were better to be married of him than of another, for he is not like to marry me well and not being well married, it will be a good excuse for me hereafter to leave my wife », 81-84). Ceci éclaire d'un jour définitif le choix qu'il a fait de Sir Oliver Martext et d'une chapelle de vert, c'est-à-dire d'une liturgie estropiée (Martext) et d'un lieu respirant le paganisme (« no temple but the wood, no assembly but horn-beasts », 44-45). On notera l'abondance de l'imagerie animale dans le discours de Touchstone sur les noces et l'amour de l'allusion à Ovide en tant que « capricious poet » (6), c'est-à-dire doué de l'instinct et de la vigueur sexuelle du bouc aux bêtes à cornes des bois témoins du mariage d'animaux promis à porter des cornes — thème qui traverse toute la pièce pour s'épanouir en chant et en spectacle allégorique dans la célébration du chasseur en 4.2 —, et aux animaux contraints par l'asservissement à l'homme ou à leur instinct : bœuf, cheval, faucon, pigeons (72-74).

La technique de Touchstone consiste à noyer d'emblée l'interlocuteur sous un flot de paroles : questions oratoires[1] (2-3) décochées à Audrey, recours à l'amplification[2] et à la gradation[3] quand il accueille Jaques (66-69) dont il se méfie comme d'un rival en bouffonnerie paré du privilège, injuste en l'occurrence, de son rang social. Touchstone joue avec les mots et en subvertit le sens par degrés. Ainsi de « wit » qui bascule dans l'obscénité du paronyme (« will » : membre viril); les mots « wit » et « will »

---

1.   Affirmation présentée sous forme de question posée de sorte à rendre la réponse superflue.
2.   Explicitation de l'affirmation d'origine.
3.   Escalade ou désescalade structurée du discours exprimant une dynamique de l'humeur.

sont associés par tradition[4] dans plusieurs expressions proverbiales. Ainsi de « poetical », et de « honest ». Comme le bouffon Feste dans *Twelfth Night*, Touchstone est un « corrupter of . . . words » parce qu'il sait, comme les gens d'autorité dont il est antinomique, la valeur performative du langage. Il plie donc le langage et le réduit à son désir. Le rythme de son discours est martelé par le recours aux polyptotes[5] : « poet », « poetry », qui éveillent en écho « poetical » dans le discours d'Audrey. « Give », « gift », « given » (61-65) constituent une autre chaîne. Il garde la parole grâce à des figures d'enchaînement imparables. Telles sont les hypophores qui marquent les lignes 45 à 57, questions qu'il se pose à lui-même pour mieux y répondre. Le jeu physique et les inflexions de la voix de l'acteur soulignent le fait qu'un des interlocuteurs favoris de Touchstone, c'est Touchstone lui-même. Par ce dédoublement de la bouffonnerie, l'autre présent en scène — Audrey dans l'instant — est récusé dans son « être là ». En Jaques, Touchstone affronte un rhéteur éprouvé ; il n'est que de voir la comparaison filée entre le mariage et la menuiserie que le mélancolique réserve au « material fool » pour enfoncer le clou au plus profond du matérialisme du bouffon.

Touchstone, confronté aux objurgations de Jaques bat en retraite derrière un ultime jeu de mots établissant Audrey et « bawdry » de manière symétrique par rapport à la ligne de partage définie par le mariage (86-87). Il veut ainsi sauver les apparences au terme d'un échange qui laissait plutôt supposer qu'Audrey et « bawdry » rimaient pour lui de manière programmatique. C'est donc une autre voix qui à la fin prévaut, tout comme c'est à la voix d'une ballade que Jaques confie son ultime message à Sir Oliver Martext. Ces phénomènes doivent être soigneusement repérés dans une pièce où les personnages choisissent fréquemment de parler d'une voix empruntée.

La parodie qui a affecté la cour faite par Touchstone à Audrey, gagne la cérémonie du mariage, ou manque de la gagner. Sir Oliver Martext, dont le nom évoque l'incompétence

---

4. Une moralité de 1568 porte le titre de *Wit and Will*. Voir aussi *AYL*, 4.1.153.
5. Formes dérivées d'un même mot.

à manier le latin, puisqu'il s'agit là de la langue liturgique dans le contexte du catholicisme romain — l'action située en terre française —, évoque les prêtres souvent campagnards du clergé récusant, peu à cheval sur les règlements, protestant à leur manière contre les contraintes imposées par la hiérarchie de la religion nouvelle. Il est possible que John Frith, recteur de la paroisse de Temple Grafton où William Shakespeare et Anne Hathaway furent peut-être unis en 1582, ait inspiré le dramaturge dans le portrait qu'il fait de Sir Oliver Martext. Au théâtre, sur les scènes modernes, Sir Oliver écorche les textes moins par ignorance du latin que par amour de la boisson. Ainsi l'arrière-plan de la grande querelle théologique du XVIᵉ siècle est-il gommé au profit d'un impact immédiat sur la salle.

Conclusion

Cette scène amorce une importante ligne structurelle de l'action dramatique : celle qui regroupe et met en perspective le mariage avorté que nous avons ici, la parodie de mariage de Rosalind/Ganymède et Orlando par Célia (4.1) et le quadruple mariage final sous les auspices païens d'Hymen. Elle équilibre le tableau de la pastorale par le personnage d'Audrey, montre Touchstone amoureux et son affrontement avec le bouffon non officiel mais efficace du monde de la pièce, Jaques. Parodie délibérément vulgaire des rites de l'amour et du mariage, elle forme un contrepoint exact à l'épisode combien plus raffiné et plus troublant joué dans 4.1 par un autre trio constitué par Rosalind, Orlando et leur témoin-prêtre Célia.

Jean-Marie MAGUIN

IX. Comparative commentary
of 4.3.92-183 and Lodge's *Rosalind*

OLIVER
    Orlando doth commend him to you both,
    And to that youth he calls his Rosalind
    He sends this bloody napkin. Are you he?

ROSALIND
    I am. What must we understand by this?   95

OLIVER
    Some of my shame, if you will know of me
    What man I am, and how, and why, and where
    This handkerchief was stain'd.

CELIA   I pray you, tell it.

OLIVER
    When last the young Orlando parted from you,
    He left a promise to return again   100
    Within an hour, and pacing through the forest,
    Chewing the food of sweet and bitter fancy,
    Lo what befell. He threw his eye aside—
    And mark what object did present itself:
    Under an oak, whose boughs were mossed with age,   105
    And high top bald with dry antiquity,
    A wretched, ragged man, o'ergrown with hair,
    Lay sleeping on his back. About his neck
    A green and gilded snake had wreathed itself,
    Who with her head, nimble in threats, approached   110
    The opening of his mouth. But suddenly
    Seeing Orlando, it unlinked itself,
    And with indented glides did slip away
    Into a bush, under which bush's shade
    A lioness, with udders all drawn dry,   115
    Lay couching, head on ground, with catlike watch
    When that the sleeping man should stir. For 'tis
    The royal disposition of that beast

To prey on nothing that doth seem as dead.
This seen, Orlando did approach the man   120
And found it was his brother, his elder brother.

CELIA
O, I have heard him speak of that same brother,
And he did render him the most unnatural
That lived amongst men.

OLIVER
And well he might so do,
For well I know he was unnatural.   125

ROSALIND
But to Orlando. Did he leave him there,
Food to the sucked and hungry lioness?

OLIVER
Twice did he turn his back, and purposed so.
But kindness, nobler ever than revenge,
And nature, stronger than his just occasion,   130
Made him give battle to the lioness,
Who quickly fell before him; in which hurtling
From miserable slumber I awaked.

CELIA   Are you his brother?

ROSALIND   Was't you he rescued?

CELIA   Was't you that did so oft contrive to kill him? 135

OLIVER
'Twas I, but 'tis not I. I do not shame
To tell you what I was, since my conversion
So sweetly tastes, being the thing I am.

ROSALIND   But for the bloody napkin?

OLIVER   By and by.
When from the first to last betwixt us two   140
Tears our recountments had most kindly bathed—
As how I came into that desert place—
I' brief, he led me to the gentle Duke,
Who gave me fresh array, and entertainment,
Committing me unto my brother's love,   145
Who led me instantly unto his cave,
There stripped himself, and here upon his arm

The lioness had torn some flesh away,
Which all this while had bled. And now he fainted,
And cried in fainting upon Rosalind.   150
Brief, I recovered him, bound up his wound,
And after some small space, being strong at heart
He sent me hither, stranger as I am,
To tell this story, that you might excuse
His broken promise, and to give this napkin,   155
Dyed in his blood, unto the shepherd youth
That he in sport doth call his Rosalind.

Rosalind faints

CELIA   Why, how now, Ganymede, sweet Ganymede!

OLIVER   Many will swoon when they do look on blood.

CELIA   There is more in it. Cousin Ganymede!   160

OLIVER   Look, he recovers.

ROSALIND   I would I were at home.

CELIA   We'll lead you thither.
(*To Oliver*) I pray you, will you take him by the arm?

OLIVER
    Be of good cheer, youth. You a man? You lack   165
    a man's heart.

ROSALIND
    I do so, I confess it. Ah, sirrah, a body would
    think this was well counterfeited. I pray you tell your
    brother how well I counterfeited. Heigh-ho!

OLIVER
    This was not counterfeit. There is too great   170
    testimony in your complexion that it was a passion of
    earnest.

ROSALIND   Counterfeit, I assure you.

OLIVER
    Well then, take a good heart and counterfeit to be
    a man.   175

ROSALIND
    So I do; but, i'faith, I should have been a woman
    by right.

CELIA

Come, you look paler and paler. Pray you, draw homewards.
Good sir, go with us.

OLIVER

That will I, for I must bear answer back   180
How you excuse my brother, Rosalind.

ROSALIND

I shall devise something; but, I pray you
commend my counterfeiting to him. Will you go?

The corresponding passage in Lodge reads thus

All this while did poor Saladyne, banished from Bordeaux
and the court of France by Torismond, wander up and down in
the forest of Arden, thinking to get to Lyons and so travel
through Germany into Italy. But the forest being full of bypaths,
and he unskillful of the country coast, slipped out of the way and
chanced up into the desert, not far from the place where
Gerismond was, and his brother Rosader.

Saladyne, weary with wandering up and down and hungry
with long fasting, finding a little cave by the side of a thicket,
eating such fruit as the forest did afford and contenting himself
with such drink as nature had provided and thirst made delicate,
after his repast he fell in a dead sleep. As thus he lay, a hungry
lion came hunting down the edge of the grove for prey and,
espying Saladyne, began to seize upon him; but seing he lay still
without any motion, he left to touch him—for that lions hate to
prey on dead carcasses—and yet desirous to have some food,
the lion lay down and watched to see if he would stir.

While thus Saladyne slept secure, fortune, that was careful
over her champion, began to smile and brought it so to pass that
Rosader—having stricken a deer that, but lightly hurt, fled
through the thicket—came pacing down by the grove with a
boar spear in his hand in great haste. He spied where a man lay
asleep and a lion fast by him. Amazed at this sight, as he stood
gazing his nose on the sudden bled, which made him conjecture
it was some friend of his. Whereupon, drawing more nigh, he
might easily discern his visage and perceived by his

physiognomy that it was his brother Saladyne, which drove Rosader into a deep passion, as a man perplexed at the sight of so unexpected a chance, marveling what should drive his brother to traverse those secret deserts without any company in such distress and forlorn sort.

Rosader's Meditation

'Now, Rosader, fortune that hath long whipped thee with nettles means to salve thee with roses and, having crossed thee with many frowns, now she presents thee with the brightness of her favors. Thou that didst count thyself the most distressed of all men mayest account thyself the most fortunate amongst men, if fortune can make men happy or sweet revenge be wrapped in a pleasing content. Thou seest Saladyne, thine enemy, the worker of thy misfortunes and the efficient cause of thine exile, subject to the cruelty of a merciless lion, brought into misery by the gods that they might seem just in revenging his rigor and thy injuries. Seest thou not how the stars are in a favorable aspect, the planets in some pleasing conjunction, the fates agreeable to thy thoughts, and the destinies performers of thy desires in that Saladyne shall die and thou free of his blood, he receive meed [reward] for his amiss [sins], and thou erect his tomb with innocent hands? Now, Rosader, shalt thou return to Bordeaux and enjoy thy possessions by birth and his revenues by inheritance. Now mayest thou triumph in love and hang fortune's altars with garlands. For, when Rosalind hears of thy wealth, it will make her love thee more willingly, for women's eyes are made of chrysocolla, that is ever unperfect unless tempered with gold, and Jupiter soonest enjoyed Danae because he came to her in so rich a shower. Thus shall this lion, Rosader, end the life of a miserable man, and from distress raise thee to be most fortunate.'

And with that, casting his boar spear on his neck, away he began to trudge. But he had not stepped back two or three paces but a new motion struck him to the very heart, that, resting his boar spear against his breast, he fell into this passionate humor: 'Ah Rosader, wert thou the son of Sir John of Bordeaux, whose virtues exceeded his valor and yet the most hardiest knight in all

Europe? Should the honor of the father shine in the actions of the son? And wilt thou dishonor thy parentage in forgetting the nature of a gentleman? Did not thy father at his last gap breathe out this golden principle: brothers' amity is like the drops of balsamum that salveth the most dangerous sores? Did he make a large exhort unto concord, and wilt thou show thyself careless? Oh Rosader, what though Saladyne hath wronged thee and made thee live an exile in the forest? Shall thy nature be so cruel, or thy nurture so crooked, or thy thoughts so savage as to suffer so dismal a revenge? What, to let him be devoured by wild beasts? Non sapit qui non sibi sapit [he is not wise who is not wise for himself] is fondly spoken in such bitter extremes. Lose not his life, Rosader, to win a world of treasure, for in having him thou hast a brother, and by hazarding for his life thou gettest a friend and reconcilest an enemy, and more honor shalt thou purchase a foe than revenging a thousand injuries.'

With that his brother began to stir and the lion to rouse himself, whereupon Rosader suddenly charged him with the boar spear and wounded the lion very sore at the first stroke. The beast, feeling himself to have a mortal hurt, leapt at Rosader and with his paws gave him a sore pinch on the breast that he had almost fallen; yet, as a man most valiant, in whom the sparks of Sir John of Bordeaux remained, he recovered himself and in short combat slew the lion, who at his death roared so loud that Saladyne awaked and, starting up, was amazed at the sudden sight of so monstrous a beast lying slain by him and so sweet a gentleman wounded.

Rosalind, ed. Donald Beecher, pp. 171-73.

The two texts reproduced above describe the same episode in narrative form, and are to be found approximately at the same stage of the story; in both recognition and conversion are closely related, though not exactly in the same sequence. Both emphasize the role of fortune, even though it is more present in Lodge. In Shakespeare, however, the reversal of fortune—the shift from fratricidal to fraternal feeling amounting to a kind of peripeteia—is complexified by the mode of narration and the theatrical graft of the napkin motif which conduces to a partial unveiling of Rosalind's disguise. The mutual recognition of the brothers (which solves the initial conflict of the play) thus leads to another form of recognition, that of Rosalind's gender. Though structurally akin in terms of plot and theme, Lodge's and Shakespeare's versions strongly differ in terms of diction and dramaturgy: Lodge's expansive and explicitly argumentative rhetoric is hardly traceable in Shakespeare's density and complexity. The comparative study of the source-text and its dramatic re-writing may thus offer possibilities of circumscribing certain writing strategies and of identifying certain operations of translation at work. One will pay particular attention to the connection Shakespeare establishes between the brothers' 'conversions' and the amorous education of Orlando.

I. Convergences

1. A temptation scene

Rosader and Orlando undergo a rite of passage, a particular kind of crisis which implies choice and dilemma. The moral debate that takes place within the hero's conscience receives however two distinct treatments, though the conflict between revenge and forgiveness is in either case rendered in almost allegorical fashion.

The theme of repentance and its corollary, forgiveness, are dramatized by Lodge in a manner reminiscent of the Morality play, with two voices presenting arguments in a formal rhetorical pattern very similar to those scenes of psychomachia in which virtues and vices competed within the theatre of the soul.

The scene of recognition, which in Greek tragedy was called anagnorisis, thus appears in both texts as a struggle within as well as a struggle against. The antiphonal nature of the debate in Lodge's novel between 'crabbed nature' and 'reformed nurture' reminds the audience of the initial monologue of Orlando in act 1, scene 1, whose subtext was evidently the traditional disputation about nature and nurture.

2. Romance

The two texts abound in characteristic features of romance: heroism, unlikely topography, exotic creatures, chance meetings, metamorphosis (Oliver as wild man), conversion of opponent to helper—Saladyne's physical exploit follows on that of Rosader; but Lodge emphasizes the miraculous aspect of the encounter with references to supernatural intuitions ('as he stood gazing, his nose on the sudden bled, which made him conjecture it was some friend of his') or to monsters ('so monstrous a beast lying slain by him'). Shakespeare's discourse adds mythical motifs like that of the snake and ostentatiously introduces that of the 'bloody napkin,' which connects the romance of male exploit and the romantic story of his love cure.

3. Sub-texts

In having Rosader or Orlando decide for the life of their villainous brother, the novel and the play both offer a Christian re-writing of the archetypal crime of Cain, where the notions of repentance, forgiveness and redemption prevail on those of retaliation, hatred and death. In introducing the snake and the antique oak, Shakespeare makes Eden and the book of Genesis still more vividly apprehensible. Also reminiscent of the Bible is the parable of the prodigal son, made explicit by Oliver in his conflictual encounter with his brother in the opening scene of the play; ironically, he is now the prodigal son who has left home and has lost his heritage, thus identifying himself with his brother's fate.

II. Departures

1. Fabula: sequence *vs.* isolation

Orlando's heroic and selfless action is the fourth act of courage—and physical violence—in Shakespeare's play; all are imputable to Orlando. Oliver is granted no heroic action; the mediation he has undertaken on behalf of his brother appears as a form of indirect and progressive confession, but he is granted no chance to redeem himself through heroic deeds as Saladyne is in the next episode of Lodge's romance. Besides, the justification for Rosalind's disguise, which is made explicit in Lodge because of the real danger of the forest, is left uncertain—if not gratuitous—in Shakespeare. In Lodge, Rosader's exploit is inscribed in a series of martial exploits: immediately after the killing of the lioness, it is Saladyne who saves Alinda from the claws of 'certain rascals that lived by prowling in the forest' who expected to kidnap the young girl in order to satisfy Torismond's lecherous appetite.

Saladyne's conversion and desire to leave France for a pilgrimage to the Holy Land precedes his chance meeting with his brother, whom he does not recognize: 'I go thus pilgrim-like to seek out my brother, that I may reconcile myself to him in all submission and afterward wend to the Holy Land to end my years in as many virtues as I have spent my youth in wicked vanities' (p. 176). Shakespeare makes Oliver's conversion and his recognition of Orlando—in both meanings of the word—coincide: purification (catharsis) and recognition (anagnorisis) are thus as close to each other as possible, as if to follow Aristotle's advice for the composition of tragedy. He has also transferred the religious conversion of Saladyne onto Duke Frederick.

2. Motifs

A first divergence concerns the physical appearance of Saladyne and that of Oliver. Saladyne's 'exterior lineaments' are those of a gentleman, while Oliver's are definitely altered. Louis Montrose argues that when Orlando confronts the 'wretched, ragged man, o'ergrown with hair' (l. 107) 'asleep amidst icons of age and antiquity, the description suggests that in confronting "his brother, his elder brother" (4.3.121), young Orlando is confronting a personification of his patriline and of the patriarchal order itself' (Montrose, 100). One may prefer to see in the features of Oliver overgrown with hair those of the 'Green Man,' or wild man—a folkloric character 'dressed up in animal skins and foliage, who brandished torches in the Midsummer pageants. He was a both frightening and comical figure and he became a popular representation of madness' (Laroque, 57).

Another striking difference concerns the motif of hunting, which appears in Lodge exclusively in this particular context: 'Rosader—having stricken a deer that, but lightly hurt, fled through the thicket—came pacing down by the grove with a boar spear in his hand in great haste.' In Shakespeare, hunting becomes a dramatic, emblematic, discursive, theatrical, and even musical theme which circulates throughout the play and from which Orlando is nearly excluded. He appears as a hunter only for his dress to be interpreted by Rosalind in the Petrarchan fashion:

> CELIA   . . . —He was furnished like a hunter—
> ROSALIND   O ominous—he comes to kill my heart. (3.2.237-8)

The motif of the 'bloody napkin' is not to be found in Lodge; nor its psychological or symbolic implication, *i.e.* Rosalind's swooning. The gift of the napkin has been viewed as 'an initiation ritual, both in martial and sexual terms . . . and the displaced version of the ceremonial "showing of the sheets" by which in some cultures a newly married woman demonstrates her virginity and fidelity to her husband. The napkin is thus a love token of a very different kind from the superficial love poems Orlando has earlier sent to Rosalind in testimony of his love' (M. Garber, 174). The 'bloody napkin' may thus be viewed as a prototype of the strawberry handkerchief in Othello.

However, the handkerchief Orlando sends as a love token 'to that youth he calls his Rosalind' (l. 93) is not merely a symbolic motif: Shakespeare makes it bridge the two stories of Oliver's conversion and Orlando's education. Hence, the sacrifice of Orlando for his brother acquires an added, sexual dimension.

Two other apparently minor departures from his source are notable in Shakespeare's text and can be related to the former accretion: first, no snake is to be found in Lodge. It is no coincidence, it seems, that this overdetermined symbol should appear in a temptation scene; nor is it surprising that the serpent should unlink itself, seeing Orlando. The allegorical meaning is redundant, and mythical figures abound under the surface of the text: Adam, Hercules, possibly Christ. Second, Lodge's explicitly male lion has become an explicitly female animal with Shakespeare, now in a specific female condition, 'with udders all drawn dry' (l. 115). The bloody napkin, the snake about to enter the man's mouth, and the hungry and threatening lioness in suck can therefore constitute a consistent line of thought of a sexual nature which doubles the surface meaning of martial exploit and exotic romance. Lodge's wholly moral concern is complicated in Shakespeare: motivations are abridged, moral discourse made elliptic, while symbols of a sexual nature appear in the guise of the snake and the lioness, the bloody napkin, and the swoonings of the male hero and his female counterpart. The respective postures of Oliver lying 'asleep on his back' (l. 108) and that of the lioness 'couching, head on ground' (l. 116) are graphically described within the space of only nine lines, in a similar position in the line and in a similar syntactic pattern; the similarity of the rhetorical pattern only pointing to a difference, *i.e.* the inversion of male and female stereotypical positions. Both the danger of the snake and the feminization of the lion are Shakespearean departures and can be read sexually: the snake about to enter the sleeping man's mouth suggests 'the threat of phallic invasion,' whereas the hungry lioness embodies the threat of being eaten, that is to say 'the possibility of female engulfment.' The twinning of the threats manifests 'the presence of two different but related kinds of danger. By overcoming the twin threats, Orlando conquers in symbolic form projections of both male and female fears' (Hayles, 66).

3. Narration

Lodge's direct narration provides few elements of commentary or distance which make the authorial voice audible—only Latin proverbs ('non sapit qui non sibi sapit') and parenthetical remarks on patterns of behaviour ('—for that lions hate to prey on dead carcasses—,' 'for women's eyes are made of chrysocolla'). On the contrary, Shakespeare makes Oliver's embassy a complex mediate procedure. Though he was the blindly asleep victim of the narrative, he appears as the omniscient narrator of his own rescue; it is in fact the narration of a narration, *i.e.* a reconstruction, an artefact. What is in Lodge the straigthforward recital of an adventure as perceived by the hero's conscience becomes in Shakespeare a narrative whose authority is in question: not only was the narrator absent from the scene he is describing—we later learn that he was the man asleep—, but also his own status as subject is blurred by the ambiguous syntax of pronouns. The narration by proxy of Orlando's action thus culminates in an act of confession and public conversion, a sort of moral stripping amounting to a symbolical rebirth as subject:

> ... in which hurtling
> From miserable slumber I awaked. (ll. 132-33)

As Louis Montrose argues in his sociological reading of the play, 'Oliver's narrative implies a casual relationship between Orlando's act of self-mastery and purgation and Oliver's "awakening"' (Montrose, 100-101). Catharsis works both ways, since 'the brothers find each other under an arbor consanguinitatis, at the de Boys "family tree"' (100).

Signs

Shakespeare has this scene of waiting twice interrupted by messengers, one already known to the cousins (Silvius bringing a letter from Phoebe), one unknown. His identity is gradually revealed, just as the theatrical sign (the napkin) has gained meaning (*i.e.* reality) in the course of the scene through the fiction of the tale: in the space of its sixty-two lines, the tale has thus translated the sign and made it effective, causing Ganymede's swooning. The visual sign—twice insistently exhibited on stage—is then framing the narrative.

The motif of the fainting is also dual: Orlando's fainting is narrated by Oliver, while Rosalind's swooning is actually staged and is later to be narrated as staged ('counterfeited'), *i.e.* fictitious. The double fainting not only raises questions about the relationship of fiction and reality, but also questions gender stereotypes: Orlando's physical strength and Rosalind's weakness are translated into the same kinetic sign—a sort of ritual exchange mediated by discourse.

Another theatrical sign must be considered, though it has no direct expression in the dramatic text: Celia and Oliver must have experienced 'love at first sight,' and this must be visually perceptible in performance. His conversion in this and the other domain may appear as instantaneous, and accords with the Christian doctrine of salvation; 'like the late-arriving labourers in the vineyard (Matt. 20:1-16) his reward is made equal to that of his apparently more deserving brother, and the two courtships, one so lengthy and the other so swift, are, in Hymen's words, "earthly things made even" (5.4.104)' (M. Garber, 175).

In the scene, Rosalind's disguise begins to slip away, her authority is partly given up, immediately after an encounter with Silvius in which she has been acting like a man and has proved to own the masculine qualities of wit and initiative. This first stage of Rosalind's unlayering is yet a scene in which the confusion of identity resorts to the ambiguities of syntax: the constant play on personal pronouns ('Are you he?') and tenses ("'Twas I, but 'tis not I') are the linguistic version of disguise, syntax as theatricality.

Another inversion of roles is noticeable, that of the dominant role between the two cousins. Celia's presence of mind keeps Rosalind's gender clear in the swooning episode, but calls Ganymede 'cousin,' instead of 'brother.' During the preceding exchanges, Rosalind has been the silent character, only absorbed in her champion's doings. Later, Rosalind's attempt at concealing her confusion and disguising it as 'counterfeiting'— *i.e.* theatricalizing reality—reaches the extreme form of layering, its extremity threatening the whole edifice of disguise previously erected by Rosalind. The irruption of prose then signals that the limits of credibility have been reached and prefigures Orlando's refusal to go on living 'by thinking' (5.2).

Rhetoric

Lodge's narrative, though teeming with picturesque, even sensational details, is in fact a heavily argumentative discourse, where he explicitly and systematically resorts to the scheme of antithesis, opposing notions like nature and nurture, natural and unnatural, revenge and reconciliation, self-centredness and selflessness; he also opposes two conceptions of legacy (the inheritance of property and that of moral qualities), of love (that of the lady and that of his brother), of worthiness (that conveyed by wealth and that conferred by personal valour). Discourse is so structurally antithetic that it comes to be organized along a proto-dramatic sequence.

On the contrary, Shakespeare's narrative is based on economy, and scarcity of developments on motivation; two lines summarize Orlando's interior debate against the two fully-developed paragraphs of 'Rosader's Meditation':

> But kindness, nobler ever than revenge
> And nature, stronger than his just occasion (ll. 129-30)

Voices

In the case of conscience the two moral voices of Rosader operate as in a psychomachia (voice A and voice B equally address the protagonist as 'you'), whereas Shakespeare has Oliver speak in two voices through a play on pronouns ('I' as simultaneously distinct from, and identical with, 'he'). The antiphonal dialectics of Rosader has thus been rewritten into the complex ventriloquism of Oliver; the proto-dramatic pattern of the moral debate has been left behind while the potentialities for disguise and ambiguity have been enhanced and pushed to their limits.

4. Shakespeare's perspective

Based on a paradox, Shakespeare's strategy here consists in a subtle play of inversions: roles, action and discourse are interchanged. For once, Orlando is not supposed to be watched, but watching:

> He threw his eye aside—
> And mark what object did present itself. (ll. 103-4)

the irony lying in that the only scene in which Orlando is not the panoptic 'object' of others is in fact mediated by someone else, thus reinstating Orlando as object (of discourse). Oliver, supposedly passive—and blind—in action, becomes active—and omniscient—in narration: conversely, Orlando, active in the exploit, is absent from the stage and the narration. The watcher and the watched thus exchange roles when it comes to verbalize—translate into words—action. Conversely, Oliver objectifies himself as he stages himself at the centre of the picture he draws.

The strategy of the gazes, or who watches whom?

Shakespeare weaves a complex maze of gazes in this staged narrative:

– first, Rosalind-as-Ganymede and Celia watch a material prop and a living person whose nature and identity are not revealed to them: they watch a spectacle whose meaning they do not command or manipulate for once; when the hearing of the tale gives a sense to the visual object presented to them, the spectacle is transferred on to the stage, with the unexpected swooning of the addressee;

– second, the unknown messenger describes Orlando watching an anonymous man: the process of recognition is twofold and differentiated, since it is first the hero of the fiction who recognizes his brother before the addressees of the narrative can interpret the play on pronouns, whose syntax has functioned as a linguistic disguise;

– third, within the fictitious world of the narrative, a concatenation of gazes operates in a transitive manner: Orlando watches the man asleep, the snake watches Orlando's watching and flees toward the grove where the lioness is 'couching . . . with catlike watch,' the lioness is watched by Orlando as she is watching Oliver;

– at the centre of the pattern, an unwitting figure, a passive object of contemplation and 'meditation'—to use Lodge's phrase—who, by a sudden about-turn, happens to be the present narrator.

The gap of awarenesses between the participants on the one hand, and between the audience and the characters on stage on the other, creates a range of complex ironies, the most evident of which on a dramatic level is the passivity and fragility of Rosalind, who, losing control, loses her role as manipulator or teacher. Peripeteia does not only concern the purgation and conversion of the two brothers; it also implies a shift of roles from the dominant, omniscient, manipulative Ganymede to the

confession that 'i' faith, I should have been a woman by right'
(ll. 176-77). A scene of plural and mutual awakening, the
temptation scene of Shakespeare's *As You Like It* is one which
screens the eye and the 'I' in a maze of gazes and pronouns.

Conclusion

Shakespeare's re-writing of Lodge's narrative, though it
resorts to the same themes and stylistic artifices, may be viewed
wholly as a complexified, theatrical translation of the source
text. Not only has Shakespeare cut short the rhetoric of the
interior debate, but he has merged the two plots of the brothers'
feud and the love cure by introducing the motif of the 'bloody
napkin.' Ganymede's swooning—also Shakespeare's
invention—pushes the limits of disguise and counterfeit to an
extreme, so that the scene may be defined not only as a fraternal
anagnorisis, but also as the first stage of Rosalind's unlayering.
Besides, it is a highly theatrical scene of 'love at first sight'
between the redeemed Oliver and Celia. The two aspects of
romance—improbable male exploit and extraordinary love
story—are thus connected by the syntax of drama, which by
adding a nexus of symbols, complexifies the romantic reading
with a consistently sexual line of thought. Symbolically as well
as discursively, Lodge's antiphonal simplicity has been rewritten into a polyphonic—*i.e.* multivocal—composition.

Pierre ISELIN

X. Concepts

anagnorisis/discovery

'A discovery [Gr. anagnorisis] is, as the very word implies, a change from ignorance to knowledge, and thus to either love or hate, in the personages marked for good or evil fortune. The finest form of discovery is one attended by reversal' (*Poetics*, 1452a30).

blazon (Fr. 'coat of arms' or 'shield')

'As a literary term it was used by the followers of Petrarchism [or Petrarchanism] to describe verses which dwelt upon and detailed the various parts of a woman's body; a sort of catalogue of her physical attributes' (J. A. Cuddon, *The Penguin Dictionary of Literary Terms*).

The recent interdisciplinary study of Jonathan Sawday, *The Body Emblazoned* (Routledge, 1995) links the display of the body in Renaissance art and literature to the activity of the great anatomists of the period.

The convention was popularized by Marot's 'Blason du beau tétin' (1536):

> Tetin refaict, plus blanc qu'un œuf,
> Tetin de satin blanc tout neuf,
> Tetin qui fait honte à la rose,
> Tetin plus beau que nulle chose,
> Tetin dur, non pas Tetin, voyre,
> Mais petite boule d'yvoire,
> Au milieu duquel est assise
> une fraise, ou une cerise . . .
> Quand on te veoit, il vient à maintz
> Une envie dedans les mains
> De te taster, de te tenir:
> Mais il se fault bien contenir
> D'en approcher, bon gré ma vie,
> Car il viendroit une autre envie . . .

and was illustrated by many Elizabethan poets, among whom Spenser (*Epithalamion*, 1595), Sidney (*Astrophel and Stella*,

1591), and Thomas Lodge (*Phillis*, 1593). Such success soon asked for parody: Shakespeare turned the blazon upside down in his famous sonnet 130:

> My Mistress' eyes are nothing like the sun,
> Coral is far more red than her lips' red:
> If snow be white, why then her breasts are dun;
> If hairs be wires, black wires grow on her head.
> I have seen roses, damask'd red and white,
> But no such roses see I in her cheeks;
> And in some perfumes is there more delight
> Than in the breath that from my mistress reeks.
> I love to hear her speak,—yet well I know
> That music hath a far more pleasing sound;
> I grant I never saw a goddess go:
> My mistress, when she walks, treads on the ground:
> And yet, by heaven, I think my love as rare
> As any she belied with false compare!

An excerpt from Marot's 'Epigramme du laid tétin' may be quoted here, as it represents the exact counterpart—or, 'contreblazon'—to the 'Epigramme du beau tétin' partly quoted above:

> Tetin qui n'as rien que la peau,
> Tetin flac, tetin de drappeau
> Grand'tetine, longue tetasse,
> Tetin, dois je dire bezasse:
> Tetin au grand villain bout noir
> Comme celuy d'un entonnoir,
> Tetin qui brimballe à tous coups
> Sans estre esbranlé, ne secous,
> Bien se peult vanter qui te taste,
> D'avoir mys la main à la paste:
> Tetin grillé, tetin pendant,
> Tetin fletry, tetin rendant
> Villaine bourbe en lieu de laict,
> Le Diable te feit bien si laid...

In *As You Like It*, Orlando's portrait of the 'quintessential' lady, this 'body . . . fill'd / With all graces wide-enlarg'd' (3.2.120-49) can be read as a form of blazoning in that the better parts of the mythical ladies mentioned are isolated, then assembled to make the perfect whole of 'Rosalinda.' This composition of parts may remind us of the legend, reported by Pliny (*Natural History*, XXV, xi) according to which Zeuxis painted a picture of Juno, and chose from the maidens of the city 'five of the fairest to take out as from severall patterns, whatsoever hee liked best in any of them; and of all the lovely parts of those five, to make one bodie of incomparable beautie' (Quoted by Agnes Latham, p. 68). Jaques alludes to the blazon in his speech of the seven ages when he pictures the lover 'Sighing like furnace, with a woeful ballad / Made to his mistress' eyebrow' (2.7.148-49).

correspondences

The mainstream discourse of the Renaissance was certainly that of correspondences, that is to say analogies between the various planes of creation. This vision that the world of nature was a prose to be read as a hieroglyph is amply documented in Foucault's *Les Mots et les Choses*, in a chapter entitled "la prose du monde." Because 'the "little world" of human nature'—or, microcosm—was 'viewed as an *epitome* of the Great world' (*OED*, art. 'microcosm'), then it was no coincidence that, for instance, the walnut and the brain 'looked alike' (to quote Crollius' famous theory of the signatures), and the former could be rightfully used to cure brain diseases. The mediaeval scheme was largely secularized by the Renaissance, which placed the 'Body Politic' between the individual 'body'—or, microcosm— and the macrocosm: just as the spheres of the universe obeyed a *primum mobile*, so the 'spheres' of society received from the sovereign—Queen Elizabeth—the impulse that made them both one and several.

Duke Senior's amused remark that

> If he [Jaques], compact of jars, grow musical,
> We shall have shorly discord of the spheres (2.7.5-6)

is precisely inspired from this theory widely drawing on neo-platonic philosophy.

courtly love

The earliest French literature—the 'troubadour' songs—either expresses the changing fortunes of fighting noblemen, or addresses a lady without peer, forever unattainable. The two themes may seem irreconcilable. In the 'Cours d'amour' of Southern France, poets actually rivalled in literary skill, displaying their ingenuity in coining new similes or in devising nice arguments. A. J. Cuddon (*The Penguin Dictionary of Literary Terms*) defines the stance that was imposed on the poet as follows: 'the lover's feelings ennoble him and make him worthier of his mistress. He longs for union with her in order to attain moral excellence.' One might rather say that through his longing for her, he is brought to seek moral excellence. By refining his discourse, he will refine his feelings to a point where it matters little that the lady—who is most often married—never will come closer to her troubadour. Courtly love is desire. It is a *school*.

disputation, [Lat. *disputatio*, discussion]

Defined in *OED* as 'the action of disputing or debating; controversial argument.' In the Middle Ages, it used to be the name of a recognised genre, one well-known instance of which is *The Owl and the Nightingale*. The two characters in turn offer statements which substantiate one of two opposing views. Taught in schools or universities, the art of *disputatio* was considered as a device by which greater knowledge of an issue could be achieved. In *As You Like It*, obvious traces of this training are visible in the organisation of discourse, as for instance the first two scenes of the play, which have one implicit, one-voiced *disputatio* over nature and nurture (1.1), and, in a more leisurely context, an explicit, two-voiced debate between Rosalind and Celia over the compared merits of nature and fortune (1.2).

euphuism

The notion is particularly relevant to the study of Shakespeare's *As You Like It* since the source text of the play is undoubtedly Thomas Lodge's romance *Rosalynde*, which claims its Lylyan lineage.

Etymology
In 1592, Gabriel Harvey, in the third of his *Four Letters and Certaine Sonnets touching Robert Greene*, coined the term from

the title of John Lyly's novel *Euphues* (see below the *Semantic approach* and the *Commentary*) in a highly polemical context as a synonym for 'bad style': 'What hee is improved since, excepting his good olde *Flores Poetarum*, and Tarletons surmounting *Rhetorique*, with a little Euphuisme, and Greenesse [*sic*] inough.' The adjective is *euphuistic*.

Semantic approach

1. Precious type of diction and style, most characteristically exemplified in John Lyly's novel *Euphues, the Anatomy of Wit* (1578) and its sequel *Euphues and his England* (1580). The main features of euphuism are traditionally described as the nearly systematic, often combined use of rhetorical questions, paronomasia, on the one hand; on the other, as the decorative or demonstrative resort to various fields of imagery—historical, mythological, natural or proverbial—generally resulting in long strings of similes all relating to the subject—the typical 'euphuism of similes' to which Gabriel Harvey so strongly objected in *Pierce's Supererogation* (1593).

2. Hence loosely applied to any kind of affected, exaggeratedly elaborate speech or writing.

3. An instance of euphuism, a euphuistic phrase or composition.

Commentary

Strikingly enough, the polemical intention which presided over the very coinage of the term in the midst of the 'Martin Marprelate Controversy' has ever since been perceptible in the derogatory connotations of 'euphuism,' as well as in the critical issues raised by Lylyan scholarship in the 1860's: whether Lyly's style was a parody of courtly diction or an innovating, creative attempt at a new prose style, whether it was imitated or ridiculed by Shakespeare, are among the quasi-ritual questions which literary criticism has often polemically tried to answer. Along with Lyly's moral or didactic intentions, the problem of the sources has generated several theories, making *Euphues* an adaptation from Guevara's *Diall of the Princes*, whose translation by North had appeared in 1557 (F. Landmann, 1880); euphuistic fashion has also been traced to Pettie's book *A Petite*

Pallace of Pettie his Pleasure, a collection of twelve stories (1576); it has in turn been traced to Queen Elizabeth's letters, to the imitations of the Classics, in particular Isocrates, Gorgias and Cicero (A. Feuillerat, 1910), to the general medieval tradition (M. W. Croll, 1916), or to John Rainold's Latin lectures (W. Ringler, 1938). Recent scholarship has explored pre-Lylyan euphuism in the aristocratic idiosyncratic style, and tended to inscribe Lyly's novels in the general 'movement of defence and illustration of the English tongue' expressed in the works of such rhetoricians as Thomas Wilson (*The Art of Rhetoric*, 1553) and Henry Peacham (*The Garden of Eloquence*, 1577).

Both traduce the continuous Tudor enthusiasm for classical rhetoric which Lyly probably shared, 'the style being the *object* of the work, what the work is about' (R. A. Lanham, 1966). It is expectedly in stylistic terms that most scholars have defined 'euphuism,' the structural devices (*e.g.*, antithesis, repetition) being generally opposed to decorative patterns (essentially similes, and allusions to history, mythology, or Pliny's 'unnatural history'). In the following example, Queen Elizabeth is the central motif of a string of natural and historical similes:

> This is she, that resembling the noble Queen of Navarre, useth the Marigold for her flower, which at the rising of the sun openeth her leaves, and at the setting shutteth them, referring all her actions and endeavours to him that ruleth the sun. This is that Caesar that first bound the Crocodile to the Palm Tree, bridling those that sought to rein her. This is that good Pelican that to feed her people spareth not to rend her own person: This is that mighty Eagle, that hath thrown dust into the eyes of the Hart, that went about to work destruction on her subjects, into whose wings although the blind Beetle would have crept, and being so carried to her nest, destroyed her young ones, yet hath she with the virtue of her feathers, consumed that fly in his own fraud.
> (*Euphues and his England*, Bond, ii, p. 215)

Though the moral and didactic intentions of such a formal rhetoric have been questioned in recent years, so far as to see *Euphues* as 'a parody of courtesy books,' and 'essentially a comic work' (T. L. Steinberg, 1977), Lyly's recurrent use of classical *schemata*—*isocolon* (= like length), *parison* (= like form), and *paromoion* (= like sound)—his preference for simile over metaphor, his 'perpetual strain after antithesis' can more safely be ascribed to his desire for rhythm and symmetry (S. Sandbank, 1971), or his pre-dramatic tendency 'to . . . present ideas from a variety of viewpoints in order to show a spectrum of possible attitudes,' thus establishing the relationship of style to the role-playing later developed in his Court Comedies, the editor of which could write in 1632: 'All our ladies were then his Schollers; And that Beautie in Court, which could not parley Euphuisme, was as little regarded, as shee which now there speakes not French.' Shakespeare echoes this aristocratic fashion of the 1580s with the patterned speeches of superfine courtiers in *Love's Labour's Lost*:

> Light seeking light doth light of light beguile:
> So, ere you find where light in darkness lies,
> Your light grows dark by losing of your eyes. (1.1.77-79)

with the balanced speech of the exiled Duke in *As You Like It*:

> And this our life, exempt from public haunt,
> Finds tongues in trees, books in the running brooks,
> Sermons in stones, and good in everything. (2.1.15-17)

or with that of Portia in *The Merchant of Venice*:

> If to do were as easy as to know what were good to do, chapels had
> been churches, and poor men's cottages princes' palaces . . . I may
> neither choose who I would, nor refuse whom I dislike, so is the will of
> a living daughter curb'd by the will of a dead father. (1.2.12-25)

The nature and amount of Shakespeare's debt to Lyly has been heavily disputed, the more so as the intertextuality can be viewed on two levels: the many characteristics of Lyly's style (bombast, verbosity, poverty of phrase and argument, excessively alliterative and repetitive patterns) which Shakespeare very certainly parodied in Falstaff's discourse on camomile: 'For though camomile, the more it is trodden on the faster it grows, yet youth, the more it is wasted the sooner it wears' (*King Henry the Fourth, Part I*, 2.4.394-97); on the other hand, the euphuistic architecture, organisation of phrase, sentence, paragraph, which largely influenced the formation of all subsequent literary prose, be it Shakespearean drama or the

1611 edition of the Bible. If then the euphuistic legacy can be assessed controversially in terms of figurative style, clockwork parallelism, and sound effect, it remains with its extraordinary density of decoration and argumentation the prototype of the axiomatic style in modern English, deeply rooted in Elizabethan proverb-lore. Such a structural filiation is to be traced in the euphuistic proverb-contest between Valentine and Proteus in the opening scene of *Two Gentlemen of Verona*.

folly/fool/clown

'folly': the range of meanings of the word is wide; as opposed to wit or wisdom, it refers to a perversity of judgment, but it may also refer to an inordinate desire; besides, as Jaques's inordinate desire for a 'motley coat' suggests, the folly of the licensed fool is the medicine which the moralist-satirist means to use to 'cleanse the foul body of th'infected world' (2.7.60). The aim of the fool's folly is precisely the wise man's folly: 'The wise man's folly is anatomized / Even by the squandering glances of the fool' (2.7.56-57).

The theatrical role of the fool is inherited from folk festivities: the fool and the Lord of Misrule are festive paradigms Shakespeare constantly drew on. The fool is thus the perpetual outsider (as he stayed outside the ordered formation of the morris dance in English festival); a representative of an alternative order, he was unromantic, libidinal and egalitarian— an alternative to the dominant order of the gentry (Wiles, 163). He may thus be viewed as an antidote to the illusion of romance. But paradoxically, the Fool in the play takes part in the final dance, as if the world of romance in its turn had contaminated that of folly.

'The clown and *idiotes* have a constant but consistent relationship to the making of the play as well as to the seeing of it. There is an association between being a clown and being on the stage, the clown, when fool, being professionally a dramatic figure, or motley to the view. . . . We notice too that the *idiotes* is often a rhetorician, and that he frequently delivers a set speech, like the speech on the seven ages of man in *As You Like It*. Just as Duke Senior's "sermons in stones" speech establishes the moral reality that keeps the pastoral convention alive in literature, so their speech, by looking at human life in terms of theatrical illusion, establishes, as in a mirror, the reality of experience that theatrical experience provides. It is thus the imaginative focus of a highly artificial comedy, where the sense of a show being put on never disappears from the action, and is not intended to do so. What fascinates us about the *idiotes* and clown is that they are not purely isolated individuals: we get fitful glimpses of a hidden world which they guard or symbolize . . . it is never a wholly simple world, and it exerts on the main action a force which is either counterdramatic or antidramatic. Some of the most haunting speeches in Shakespeare are connected with these shifts of perspective provided by alienated characters' (N. Frye, 100-101).

Kempe or Armin?

Will Kempe left the Chamberlain's Men early in 1599. For Robert Armin, his successor, Shakespeare wrote jester's parts like that of the Fool in *King Lear,* Lavatch in *All's Well That Ends Well*, Feste in *Twelfth Night*, and Trinculo in *The Tempest.* Armin had a reputation as musician and singer, so that one has been tempted to attribute the role of Touchstone to the more musical of Shakespeare's Fools. In terms of chronology, both Kempe and Armin might have played the role. But it remains surprising that, in a play which is filled with songs, none is given to the jester: Amiens sings, so do the pages in 5.3, but does Touchstone actually sing when he leaves Sir Oliver Martext in 3.3?

fortune

A legacy from classical Rome, the goddess *Fortuna* remained familiar over the midle-ages, probably through the agency of an allegorical representation found in Cicero's *Somnium Scipionis.* The dreamer there sees a Lady moving a great wheel, on which characters, the representatives of the various 'estates' (social conditions), in turn are raised and brought down. The same wheel appears in Boethius' *Consolatio Philosophiae*, a book that met wide audiences in mediaeval England, and finds its way into English literary tradition. A famous instance is Malory's *Morte d'Arthur*, where the Lady and her wheel appear, also for the benefit of the *dreaming* Arthur.

The most striking characteristic of the Lady Fortune is her fickleness—to the mediaeval man, a symbol of mutability, a scourge inflicted on our sublunary world: this feature is symbolized by the wheel, and also by the fact that the lady is often blindfolded, and therefore acts without a purpose. Such a representation however challenged the christian concept of 'Providence,' which may acount for the ambivalent status of a symbol that was known truly to represent human condition, yet had lost its awe-inspiring aspect, and could be toyed with.

A Renaissance, more active, conception of fortune is also present in the play, as can be seen in the juxtaposition of the two acceptations in the same context. Fortune as chance, opportunity, is present both as the leading concept of Lodge's romance (see the passage studied) and as one alternative conception of fortune. Present in the discourse of nearly all the exiled characters, it appears as a court topos, alternately derided by the princesses ('the good housewife Fortune,' 1.2.30) and taken seriously by Duke Senior when he praises the virtues of this forest life which protects them from the buffets and the 'stubbornness' of fortune (2.1.12-20).

green world

Named by Northrop Frye from Keats' *Endymion*, 1.16, 'the forest or green world, then, is a symbol of natural society, the word natural here referring to the original human society which is the proper home of man, not the physical world he now lives in but the "golden world" he is trying to regain. This natural society is associated with things which in the context of the ordinary world seem unnatural, but which are in fact attributes of nature as a miraculous and irresistible reviving power. These associations include dream, magic and chastity or spiritual energy as well as fertility and renewed natural energies. Magic in Shakespeare's day was an "art," and we have seen that arts, especially music, are also attributes of a world which, being natural for man, is a world in which art and nature are at one' (N. Frye, 142-43).

happy ending

'A comedy is not a play which ends happily: it is a play in which a certain structure is present and works through to its own logical end, whether we or the cast or the author feel happy about it or not. The logical end is festive, but anyone's attitude to the festivity may be that of Orlando or of Jaques's' (N. Frye, 46).

humour

Inherited from ancient and mediaeval physiology, 'humour' named each of the four fluids that were supposed to govern the disposition of the body. Just as the four elements in macrocosm combined hot or cold with moist or dry, so did the four humours—blood, phlegm, choler and melancholy—within the microcosm of man's body. In the Elizabethan age, the word 'humour' had spread beyond this technical—medical—sense, and 'sanguine,' 'phlegmatic,' 'choleric,' or 'melancholy' were broadly used to describe a man's dominant mood. As such, humour was a theme for literary treatment. See Ben Jonson's comedies *Every Man in his Humour* (1598) and *Every Man out of his Humour* (1599). See also 'melancholy.'

masque

Perhaps derived from dances in which the disguised—and masked—performers assumed roles, the dramatic genre flourished as courtly entertainment in the Renaissance, especially in the reigns of Elizabeth I, James I and Charles I. It combined music, dance, song and drama—that is, it included spoken dialogue, mostly concerned with mythological subjects, and always ended with a dance. 'In short, it was a kind of elegant, private pageant' (Cuddon, *The Penguin Dictionary of literary terms*).

With Ben Jonson and Inigo Jones, masque performance reached an extreme degree of sophistication—resorting to rich costumes, elaborate sets and spectacular stage machinery. It had also become extremely expensive, and its career met with a sudden end when the puritans closed the theatres.

The masque however was to be a source not only for musical comedy, but also for the opera. Shakespeare borrows from the masque, for instance as he includes the masque of Juno and Ceres within the fourth act of *The Tempest*.

The masque of Hymen in *As You Like It* is the necessarily pagan alternative of the wedding ritual which could not be performed on a stage.

melancholy/malcontent,

Hamlet—the English theatre's most durable portait of the melancholic man—'demonstrates the ideological potential of basing a character on theories of melancholy' (Heffernan, 97).

The composition of the comic figure of Jaques, like that of Hamlet, must have been influenced by medical treatises, in particular Timothy Bright's *A Treatise of Melancholie* (1586), much in vogue between 1586 and 1613. Robert Burton's *The Anatomy of Melancholy* and Jacques Ferrand's *Erotomania* came too late to have influenced Shakespeare's conception of Jaques.

Broadly defined as a temperamental hypersensitivity and thoughtfulness, melancholy is the 'Elizabethan malady.'

In *Voices of Melancholy* (1971), Bridget Lyons examines the relation between melancholy as a humour and its literary treatment at the end of the sixteenth century: 'Melancholy was classified as a disease, condemned as a vice, or exalted as the condition and symptom of genius. But all these different traditions about melancholy expressed, implicitly, the idea if its social importance—it was a physical and psychological condition that expressed an orientation towards the world and society—and this made it particularly susceptible to literary treatment.'

Critics have tried to identify Jaques to contemporary satirists. Jaques knows in advance that it will be hard to make the world take his medicine; this is why he plans to 'shoot his wit' under cover of the motley coat. In its feebler forms the pastoral tends to escapism and sentimentality; in its more serious manifestations, it has affinities with satire.

If he sometimes proves to be antisocial and if his nature is contemplative, Jaques is mostly seen in company, and talking. The images and ideas associated with Jaques's melancholy in the play are: the weeping stag, solitude, time, exclusion from love, and travel. The definition he gives of his condition makes it an individual type of melancholy (4.1.10-20).

In this passage, Jaques expresses the pervasiveness of melancholy, at the same time as he parodies 'the elaborate classifications of the varieties of melancholy found in the popular medical treatises of the day' (98). The reference he makes to 'simples' and 'humorous' echoes the theory of the day: 'melancholy is either simple or mixed . . .' (Burton). The melancholic humour is in his case related to 'rumination,' 'contemplation' and 'travel.'

William Richardson, an eighteenth-century scholar, in discussing Jaques's nature, distinguished between melancholy and misanthropy: 'On comparing the sorrow excited by repulsed and languishing affection, with that arising from the disappointment of selfish appetites melancholy appears to be the temper produced by the one, misanthropy by the other. Both render us unsocial; but melancholy disposes us to complain, misanthropy to inveigh' (*A Philosophical Analysis and Illustration of Some of Shakespeare's Remarkable Characters*, 1784, p. 56). He judges the character of Jaques to be a 'mixture of melancholy and misanthropy.'

John Charles Bucknill (1817-1897) describes Jaques's melancholy as 'the result of matured intellect and exhausted desire. Jaques is an "old man," or at least old enough to be called so by the rustic lass in her anger of disappointment, and he himself attributes his melancholy to his wide knowledge of the world' (*The Mad Folk of Shakespeare*, 1868, p. 292). Another nineteenth-century commentator has seen Jaques as representing 'a certain delicate shade of incipient melancholia . . . a species of intellectual and emotional epicurean' (Kellogg). He finds in him the 'gentle satirist.'

Lawrence Babb, in *Elizabethan Malady* (1951), labels Jaques 'the best example in the drama of the malcontent in the role of philosophic critic' (93). Helen Gardner (1968) views Jaques as 'the cynic, the person who prefers the pleasures of superiority, cold-eyed and cold-hearted' (66-67), while Erwin Panofsky considers that he 'uses the mask of a melancholic by fashion and snobbery to hide the fact that he is a genuine one' (*Albrecht Dürer*, 1.166).

Hardin Craig, in his introduction to *As You Like It*, expresses the paradoxical view that 'Jaques does nothing and yet is indispensable.'

In sympathizing with the weeping stag and translating the spectacle 'into a thousand similes' (2.1.45), Jaques proves to fit Bright's description of the melancholic as of great understanding and imagination: 'Sometimes it falleth out, that melancholic men are found verie wittie, and quickly discerne: either because the humour of melancholie with some heate is so made subtile, that as from the driest woode risest the clearest flame' (Bright, 130). For this reason Duke Senior loves 'to cope him in these sullen fits, / For then he's full of matter' (2.1.67-69). Winfried Schleiner, in an article entitled 'Jaques and the Melancholy Stag' (*English Language Notes* 17, 1980), has shown how the stag, defined as cold and dry, shared characteristics with the melancholic, and how its tears (known as *lapis bezoar*) had medicinal value to cure melancholy.

Jaques's withdrawal from the court is not only a political exile; it suggests rather 'the hermit's withdrawal to the desert' (Heffernan, 107). The desire for solitude and dark places is a common symptom of the malady. This alienation may lead to thought, reading and writing; it may more probably lead to vanity and idleness—*acedia*.

Another central concern to the play and to melancholy is time. Jaques's famous disquisition on the seven ages of man (2.7.139-66) presents 'the seven-act play of life as pointless and absurd. . . . The passage culminates in two protracted descriptions of the stages of old age and senility' (110-11). Jaques's choice of exile has been variously interpreted. For W. H. Auden, it is spiritual; for William P. Shaw ('Sense and Staging in Shakespeare's Comedies: Jaques and [the] Wedding dance,' in *The Laurel Bough*, 25-53. Ed. by G. Nageswara Rao. Bombay: Blackie & Sons, 1983), it is 'the crowning expression of his egocentricity' (28), he has 'rejected the organic perspective and embraced its antithesis—one which precludes growth, interdependency in community, toleration, equilibrium, purpose, joy and love, or any prospect for renewal. Rather than dance to the rhythms of life "with measures heaped in joy," Jaques opts out: "I am other than for dancing measures"' (29).

Though taking a trip was thought therapeutic, 'travel seems to be at least the partial cause of the malady' (Heffernan, 117): 'the sundry contemplation of my travels, in which [my] often rumination wraps me in a most humorous sadness' (4.1.17-20). Duke Senior's attack on Jaques's libertinism (2.7.66-68) certainly draws on the commonplace idea that 'the continent will have tempted the traveller into sexual indulgence, which, in turn, frequently led to dejected spirits or worse' (118-10).

Shakespeare's treatment of melancholy in the comedy of *As You Like It* may be seen as light and humorous; his tragic portrait of melancholy in *Hamlet* is of a much darker and deeper kind.

metaphor (Gr. 'to transfer'; Fr. métaphore)

An abridged form of comparison in which the first term or 'tenor' (Fr. comparé) is removed, leaving only the second term or 'vehicle' (Fr. comparant). [The terms 'vehicle' and 'tenor' were first used by I. A. Richards]. Where simile offers a fully visible parallel between the element of reality discussed and its proposed analogy, metaphor offers a poetic alternative, a substitute for reality or the accepted norm. Metaphor may be contained in a single word or else expanded (Fr. filée), sometimes to the point of systematic development which is found in conceit. Concatenated metaphors derived from discrepant levels of thought or reality are called mixed metaphors. These constitute a vice of language and thought; their effect may be comical. Generally speaking metaphors signal a desire or a dread of metamorphosis. Translation, metamorphosis, metempsychosis are related forms of transformation in the Ovidian context of *As You Like It*.

motley

Whether the word points to the pattern it carries, or to the material it is made of, the 'motley (coat)'—'full of stolen patches, and yet never a patch like one other' (Dekker, quoted by S. Trussler, *Shakespearian Concepts*)—emblematises its wearer as 'the fool.' See Folly.

nature

Schmidt Lexicon, art. 'Nature' (usually feminine, sometimes neuter)

1) the world around us as created and creating by fixed and eternal laws. *AYL* 2.4.56. 3.2.149.

Denoting spontaneous growth and formation: *AYL* 1.1.18

Opposed to fortune: *AYL* 1.2.43, 45.

Opposed to human institutions or tendencies (law of nations) Implying the idea of necessity.

2) native sensation, innate and involuntary affection of the heart and mind: *AYL* 4.3.130.

3) the physical and moral constitution of man:

AYL 2.4.56 'So is all nature in love mortal in folly'

4) individual constitution, personal character: *The Tempest* 4.188 'on whose nature nurture can never stick.'

5) quality, sort, kind:

AYL 3.1.16 'let my officers of such a nature make an extent upon his house'

6) human life, vitality.

'The mythical or primitive basis of comedy is a movement toward the rebirth and renewal of the powers of nature, this aspect of literary comedy being expressed in the imagery more directly than in the structure' (N. Frye, 119).

onomastics

Onomastics is the study of names, and especially of their origins. For instance, one name chosen by one of the characters is anything but fortuitous, as it refers to a well-known myth associated with homosexuality:

'Ganymedes: a beautiful youth of Phrygia, son of Tros, and brother of Ilus and Assaracus. According to Lucan, he was son of Dardalus. He was taken up to heaven by Jupiter as he was hunting, or rather tending his father's flocks on mount Ida, and he became the cup-bearer of the gods in the place of Hebe. Some say that he was carried away by an eagle, to satisfy the shameful and unnatural desires of Jupiter. He is generally represented sitting on the back of a flying eagle in the air (Virg., *Aen.* 5, v, 252; Ovid, *Metam.* 10, v, 155).'

(Lemprière, *Classical Dictionary*, 3rd edition, London: Routledge, [1788]-1984).

A corrupt form of 'Ganymede,' the noun 'catamite' ('a boy kept for natural purposes,' *OED*) passed into English.

paradox

'paradoxe: Opinion contraire à l'opinion commune, affirmation qui, au premier abord, paraît choquante, mais qui, à la réflexion, est conforme à la réalité [...] On rapprochera le paradoxe de l'oxymore. Tous deux réveillent l'attention en heurtant l'intelligence. Tous deux brusquent le lecteur pour qu'il ouvre les yeux' (Henri Morier, *Dictionnaire de poétique et de rhétorique*).

pastoral

1. context

Theocritus, *Idylls* (3rd century B.C.)

Virgil, *Bucolics* (40 B.C.)

Ariosto, *Orlando Furioso* (transl. John Harrington, 15)

Edmund Spenser, *The Shepherd's Calendar*, 1574

John Lyly, *Gallathea*, performed in 1584-89

Sir Philip Sidney, *The Old Arcadia* (1577-1580), published only in 1926; *New Arcadia* (1590-93)

Thomas Lodge, *Rosalynde* (1590)

2. structure

The world of the pastoral is implicitly one of opposition between nature and culture, court and rural life, otium and negotium. Its didactic intentions appear in the moralizing conclusions reached through comparisons. Convention has it that pastoral life is sweeter than the less authentic life of the court, but Touchstone asserts the superiority of home and comfort: 'When I was at home, I was in a better place' (2.4.15), thus reverting the meaning of 'better place' used by Le Beau to refer to the Green World.

The unique theme of this genre is the love of shepherds and shepherdesses, which explains its discursive character. Leo Salingar aptly defined *As You Like It* as 'a discussion play or symposium.'

The structure of the play, with its alternation of duets, poems, debates and songs, its dearth of theatrical scenes, and of 'events linked together by the logical intricacies of cause and effect' (H. Jenkins) implies not only that 'its scenes have a pastoral genealogy, but also that they retain a pastoral character' (Paul Aspers, 71).

From Act 2 onwards, all the scenes except three (2.2, 2.3, 3.1) take place in the forest of Arden, which can at least partly be viewed as the setting of the pastoral, even though limits and frontiers have to be considered within the world of Arden. The setting of the play is the object of multiple interpretation. Viewed from the court by Charles the wrestler, the Forest of Arden appears as a romantic, even mythical place, where Duke Senior and his followers live peaceably in a new golden age or an earthly paradise (1.1.109-13). Because it is a universe overdetermined by fiction, Arden is ultimately a scene-within-the-scene, a theatrical space (Shakespeare's wooden 'O') where everyone plays his role. *Totus mundus agit histrionem* was the Globe's motto, and the play's recurrent motif. Also the heart of the forest is associated with magic:

– the figure of the circle appears at least twice with Jaques (2.5.55) and Orlando (5.4.32-34);

– one can find a form of angelic pastoralism in the conversion of both villains—Oliver wants to become a shepherd (4.3.134-38), and Duke Frederick abandons all his possessions and renounces the world (5.4.155-57);

– the play closes on Hymen's masque, prompted by Ganymede-Rosalind's magic, which gives relativity to what the pastoral episode had created.

Arden can therefore be viewed as neither the traditional pastoral world, nor the natural wilderness, neither as the exact mirror of the court, nor an inverted mirror of the court. Its ambiguous topography is suggested in the description of Ganymede and Aliena's sheepcote, which stands 'in the purlieus of this forest' (4.3.77), that is to say in an interstitial place, on the edge of the forest, near a river, an intermediate space between the world of polity and the forest's sanctuary.

The Duke and his followers have adopted pastoral as a life-style and a style of its own—*i.e.* a verbal means of expression.

The 'translation' of Fortune's buffets into a style adapted to the rules of the pastoral tradition underlines the strong connection between the pastoral and language. As he impersonates a pastoral character, the Duke speaks the language of the pastoral poet, interprets the language of nature (2.1.12-20). Similarly, Orlando's amorous rhetoric textualizes the forest (3.2.1-10). Here in the form of a truncated sonnet, Orlando repeats the traditional gesture of the pastoral lover, *i.e.* carving poems on trees. He too translates (into words) the pastoral universe. The Shakespearean pastoral of Arden is so literalized that its artificiality is conspicuous. The rustic characters William and Audrey, Corin, Phoebe and Silvius—all typify respectively wisdom, common sense, and pastoral love. Silvius's discourse (2.4.30-40), with its 'if' refrain and song-like structure, belongs to the pure tradition of the eclogue, and is parodied by Touchstone immediately afterwards (2.4.43-52), in a style which alternates the mock-heroic (characterized by elevated style and trivial subject) and the gross realism of bawdy allusions (the reading of peascod as codpiece is part of the double-entendre).

The duet of Phoebe and Silvius (3.5.8-35)—a play-within-the-play—is likewise a set piece treated in Petrarchan idiom inherited from Lodge. Here 'they take their conventional language and their conventional feelings seriously, with nothing in reserve. As a result, they seem naive and rather trivial' (C. L. Barber, *Shakespeare's Festive Comedy*). During this exchange, Phoebe literalizes the tropes of Silvius's Petrarchan rhetoric (3.5.10-20); she thus empties the poetic diction and deconstructs the poetic ventriloquism of Silvius.

3. Pastoral and anti-pastoral

The dark pastoral of the forest of Arden has nothing of edenic plenty; it takes place in a postlapsarian world, where business and corruption plague the shepherds' lives (2.4.70-86), where the forest proves cruel and dangerous, cold and 'uncouth' (2.6.6)—even if it is a 'civilized wilderness' (Marienstras, *Le Proche et le lointain*)—, where good manners assuage the hardships of this life. A world in which hunting is necessary—even if the killing of animals does not inhere in the spirit of the pastoral. Hence Jaques's moody meditation on the death of the deer (2.1.25-66) as reported by the First Lord. Hunting and a melancholic's response to it are thus anti-pastoral motifs embedded within the pastoral and contribute to deconstruct the convention by a strategy of disguise—the stereopype of the pastoral moralist moralizing on the pseudo-pastoral life of Arden in terms of the polity. Because the codes of the pastoral are so ostentatious and the artificiality of the forest so conspicuous, Arden may thus be viewed as both factitious and fictitious: 'we are invited to view the pastoral convention simultaneously from the inside, as in Lodge, and from the outside, as a frankly artificial and illusory construction' (Young). It relates to the notion of nature insofar as it is a place of redemption, regeneration and discovery, also of freedom; hence a place where human nature is redeemed. This country of the mind is one from which characters must return to the real world. 'Arden is a meeting place of Art and Nature,' as David Palmer argues, and the relationship between them is ultimately reconciled as nature is discovered through Art.

Petrarchanism (or Petrarchism)

In a broad sense the imitation of Petrarch's style in poetry, particularly its use of antithesis, paradox, oxymoron and conceit. Petrarch (1304-74), the author, among many other learned works, of the *Triomfi* and the *Canzoniere*, was considerably plagiarized and imitated during and after his life and he had a considerable influence on European poets: Bembo, Michelangelo, Tasso, Ronsard, du Bellay, Lope de Vega, Gongora, Camoëns, Wyatt, Surrey, Sidney, Spenser and Shakespeare (and some other Elizabethans). (Adapted from J. A. Cuddon, *A Dictionary of Literary Terms*).

Yet the influence of Petrarchanism should not be overestimated, as has been done for long whenever an oxymoron or the association of grief and joy in love appeared. V. Saulnier, in his thesis on Maurice Scève (1948), is right in deflating this monopoly: 'A force de gonfler, si j'ose dire, l'influence du pétrarquisme, on donnerait à penser que ce fut un phénomène littéraire à part; qu'il offusqua, au point de la faire oublier, toute tradition de poésie amoureuse. Rien ne serait plus faux. Il n'est rien de plus mêlé, en ses sources, et de plus impur, que cette psychologie et cette phraséologie d'antithèse de l'amour doux amer, auxquelles on donne libéralement, dans la poésie de la Renaissance, l'étiquette de pétrarquisme.' In particular, one has to be very cautious in textual approaches, as the rhetoric of the Canzoniere may well express feelings or ideas—neo-platonic for instance—which are radically opposed to Petrarchanism.

What characterizes Petrarchanism—though it is presumptuous to give one reading of such an opaque, adaptable text mediated by so many imitators, commentators and adaptators—is the inscription of erotic desire in poetic language. But Petrarchanism, like courtly love, has political implications, and 'was adapted to very political purposes, especially in England, where the fact of a Virgin Queen on the throne reproduced an extraordinary transference of the Petrarchan manner to politics . . . In Petrarch's own work, the relationship between the poet and his beloved seems to reflect the uneasy reorganization of feudal class relations: Laura is the suzerain, her poet the vassal, eager to follow her, yet aware of his unworthiness and the hopelessness of his attaining her. In the same way, the political relations of the Elizabethan Court were articulated through Petrarchism' (Gary Waller, *English Poetry of the Sixteenth Century*). As to the particulars of the Petrarchan system, its most crucial characteristic is the contrast between the mistress's fair outside and her icy or stony heart which inevitably causes the lover suffering; achievement, consummation, are unthinkable, though the permanent preoccupation of the lover:

'But what Petrarchanism focuses on is not these physical characteristics per se, but their effect on the lover. Typically, it is expressed as masochism—as cruelty, disease, distress, and pain. The lady's effects upon the lover are like fire, ice, blindness, mischief, instability, and yet the lover is inevitably drawn to her, puzzled over his self-torture. And, in particular, it is the combination of such effects which characterizes the peculiar impasse of Petrarchan love. It is, together, frustration balanced by hope, the love of God by the love of the world, time by fame, passivity by restlessness, public by private, coldness and ice by fire . . . Absence is a seeming necessity; presence is not conducive to poetry' (*ibid.*).

The absent Petrarchan mistress is entirely the product of the discourse in which she is placed. Another major characteristic of Petrarchan love is that, while the mistress is unapproachable, and her lover is spurred on by his suffering, he, as poet, projects his desires into a theatre of his own, one in which he takes the active role and in which the woman is assigned silent, iconic functions. The invisibility of Rosalind, her absence from the forest where Orlando is anxious to meet her in the guise of Ganymede, are then theatrical developments on the theme of Petrarchan love.

The ritual carving of the beloved's name and love sonnets is a well-known conceit in the Renaissance, and represents an oblique mode of iconism—the name becoming the object of a cult—as illustrated in the episode of Angelica and Medoro, in Ariosto's *Orlando Furioso*:

'Among so many pleasures, whenever a straight tree was seen shading a fountain or clear stream, she had a pin or knife ready at once' (trans. Lee, 1977, pp. 29-30).

primogeniture

1) Condition of being the first-born child.
2) The right of succession belonging to the first-born.

The authority on the subject is certainly Louis Adrian Montrose (see bibliography). See also Anny Crunelle-Vanrigh, '"At-one together": les liens du sang...comme il vous plaira,' in *Lectures d'une œuvre. As You Like It de William Shakespeare,* Ouvrage coordonné par Maurice Abiteboul, Editions du Temps, Paris, 1997, pp. 51-67.

poet/poetry

Touchstone's mock-defense of poetry (3.3.14-18) is articulated on the polysemy of the English 'feign' (*i.e.* lie and invent):

A passage in Sir Philip Sidney, *A Defence of Poetry* develops the topos:

'[ii. poets are liars] . . . I truly think, that of all writers under the sun the poet is the least liar, and, though he would, as a poet can scarcely be a liar. . . now, for the poet, he nothing affirms, and therefore never lieth. For, as I take it, to lie is to affirm that to be true which is false . . . But the poet never affirmeth . . . And therefore, as in history, looking for truth, they may go away full fraught with falsehood, so in poesy, looking but for fiction, they shall use the narration but as an imaginative ground-plot of a profitable invention' (ed. J. A. Van Dorsten, O.U.P., 1966, pp. 52-53).

peripeteia/reversal of fortune,

The Greek word means 'sudden change,' from prosperity to ruin, and refers to a reversal of fortune. It is used by Aristotle in his *Poetics*, and there exemplified from *Oedipus*: 'here the opposite of things is produced by the messenger, who, coming to gladden Oedipus and to remove his fears as to his mother, reveals the secret of his birth' (*Poetics*, chap. VI).

prelapsarian

The adjective was used by mediaeval theologians to point to the happy condition man enjoyed before the fall—still exempt from the guilt of the original sin (lat. *lapsus*).

romance

The word's spectrum of meaning is wide and inclusive, even in its strictly Elizabethan use. What we expect to find under such a heading is distance, social remoteness and noble antiquity, surprising events, adventure, together with an exaggeration of certain traits of human behaviour in matters of love and sexuality. Romantic imagination idealizes, or even spiritualizes sex, as is recurrently illustrated in the Petrarchan posture [see Petrarchanism]. The regular ingredients of Elizabethan romance, according to Pettet (*Shakespeare and the Romance Tradition*, 1949) are love as source of poetry and imagination, courtship, conversion of the lover's dejection into well-turned sonnets, the poet's contempt for 'flesh's frail infection' and his exaggeration of the lady's physical beauty. As narrative, romance is based on incident rather than on intrigue; on unlikely heroic events, marvellous, fabulous beasts, far-fetched adventures, magic, disguises, mistaken identities, lack of recognition. All this we find in *As You Like It*, but not uncritically rendered.

Rosalind is a complex case of cross-dressing as the persona undergoes a four-fold tranformation. The romantic code is therefore strained to an extreme 'suspension of disbelief.' But the mask hardly conceals the face under it, as several riddling allusions are hints of the truth. This built-in irony does not inhere in the world of romance. Neither does the constant framing of the romantic scenes, which are either overheard, criticized, parodied, or echoed throughout the play.

The romantic conventions are thus regularly questioned or contrasted in *As You Like It*: the romantic conventions of love at first sight, amorous furor become objects of spectacle, if not altogether of derision. The actors are aware of the folly of their romantic postures:

> If thou rememb'rest not the slightest folly (2.4.31)
> Most friendship is feigning, most loving, mere folly (2.7.182)

Orlando is regularly perceived as fool or madman: either as Orando furioso, or as Orlando inamorato. There is such a thing as a folly of romance in a play where the hero accepts to play the apparently absurd love game of courting a substitute (male) figure instead of his Rosalind.

satire/satyr

'Depuis Juvénal, les poètes satiriques sont les zélateurs d'une Muse qui n'existait pas avant eux: l'Indignation' (Victor Hugo, *Châtiments*, introduction).

'Satire,' from the Latin 'satura,' a medley, first referred to often disrespectful commentaries of men and manners (especially prominent men and public affairs). Social and moral criticism thus was provided with a special poetic genre, illustrated by Horace—a mild critic—or by Juvenal—a much harsher one. Imitation of the classics in the Renaissance brought the genre new relevance, and new developments, whether mild or harsh, as for instance Erasmus's *Moriae Encomium* (1509), or in Elizabethan drama, Marston's *The Malcontent* or most of Ben Jonson's comedies.

In Elizabethan England, the word 'satire' was wrongly connected with 'satyr,' a Greek word meaning 'woodland demon' and represented as a hybrid of man and goat in Renaissance iconography. The association was made all the easier because the Greeks performed mythological 'satyr-plays'; the wrong etymology thus led to connecting the representation of rural, 'natural' life with the 'satire' that pointed out to the wrongs and evils of 'civilisation.' In *As you Like It*, the two strands of meaning resulting from this double etymology can be identified and are merged into the 'mild' satire of the melancholic who 'pierceth through / The body of country, city, court' (2.1.58-59) and the licensed fool, who 'uses his folly like a stalking horse, and under the presentation of that he shoots his wit' (5.4.101-102).

set speech

In drama, 'set speech' is a term loosely assigned to any form of self-contained monologue, as detached from dialogue. In a more precisely rhetorical sense, 'set speech' refers to report, retrospective deliberation, plan. Such set speeches, already present in Seneca's plays, could contribute facts relevant to the play, yet not staged (retrospects, events supposed to have happened in a distant place, etc.), or the character's private thoughts and feelings, whether in the making of a plan for action, in the analysis of action already taken, or at some turning point in the plot. Wolfgang Clemen (quoted by Simon Trussler, *Shakespearean Concepts*) credits Shakespeare with the way in which 'the formal set speech gradually becomes possessed of dramatic life.'

signatures (Doctrine of)

'The belief that the distinguishing features of a plant (its colouring, shape, etc.) indicated its appropriate use in herbal medicine. Thus the yellow saffron was used for bilious attacks, while Canterbury bells, being long-necked, were supposedly good for sore throats' (Simon Trussler, *Shakespearean Concepts*). See also correspondences.

theatrum mundi

Another symbolical representation of the world, that equates it with a theatre, 'suggesting that the world is a kind of theatrical representation in the mind of God' (Simon Trussler, *Shakespearean Concepts*), to which again the player's theatre stands as a microcosm.

theophany

From the Greek: appearance of God. 'Theological term for the appearance of a god, or the celebrations thereof. It is sometimes found in critical usage to describe such an appearance in a play' (Simon Trussler, *Shakespearean Concepts*).

Pierre ISELIN

Essential bibliographical references

Commented Bibliography

WELLS, Stanley ed., *Shakespeare: A Bibliographical Guide*, new edition (Oxford: Clarendon Press, 1990)

Source (Lodge's in modern transcription)

LODGE, Thomas, *Rosalind,* ed. Donald BEECHER (Ottawa: Dovehouse Editions, 1997).

On 'romance'

BEER, Gillian, *The Romance*, The Critical Idiom (Methuen, 1970), ch. 1, 'History and Definition,' and 2, 'Medieval to Renaissance Romance: History and Myth,' pp. 1-38.

PETTET, E. C., *Shakespeare and the Romance Tradition* (1949; Methuen, 1970), pp. 122-32.

PHIALAS, Peter G., *Shakespeare's Romantic Comedies* (University of North Carolina Press, 1966), pp. 209-55.

SCOUFOS, Alice-Lyle, "The *Paradiso Terrestre* and the Testing of Love in *As You Like It*," *Shakespeare Studies*, 14 (1981), 215-27.

On comedy, ritual, anthropological approaches

FRYE, Northrop, *A Natural Perspective: The Development of Shakespearean Comedy and Romance* (Columbia UP/Harcourt, Brace and World, 1965), *passim.*

BARBER, C. L., *Shakespeare's Festive Comedy* (Princeton UP, 1959), pp. 222-39 and *passim.*

LAROQUE, François, *Shakespeare's Festive World* (CUP, 1991), *passim.*

LAROQUE, François, "Ovidian Transformations and Folk Festivities in *A Midsummer Night's Dream, The Merry Wives of Windsor*, and *As You Like It*," *Cahiers Elisabéthains*, n° 25 (Avril 1984), 23-36.

On comedy as a genre

SALINGAR, Leo, *Shakespeare and the Traditions of Comedy* (CUP, 1974), *passim*. Especially pp. 287-99.

SCRAGG, Leah, *Shakespeare's Mouldy Tales: Recurrent Plot Motifs in Shakespearian Drama* (Longman, 1992). Especially ch. 2, 'Gender Exchange,' et 5, 'Exile.'

On Pastoral

YOUNG, David, *The Heart's Forest, A Study of Shakespeare's Pastoral Plays*, New Haven and London: Yale University Press, 1972.

LASCELLES, Mary, "Shakespeare's Pastoral Comedy," in *More Talking of Shakespeare*, ed. John Garrett (Longmans, 1959), pp. 70-86.

ASPERS, Paul, *What is Pastoral*, University of Chicago Press, 1996.

Emblematic reading

BATH, Michael, "Weeping Stags and Melancholy Lovers: The Iconography of *As You Like It*," *Emblematica*, 1 (1986), 13-52.

On the fool, on satire and melancholy

HEFFERNAN, Carol Falvo, *The Melancholy Muse*, Duquesne University Press, 1995, chap. IV, pp. 95-120.

BENNETT, Robert B., "The Reform of a Malcontent: Jaques and the Meaning of *As You Like It*," *Shakespeare Studies*, 9 (1976), 183-204.

DILLON, Janette, *Shakespeare and the Solitary Man* (Macmillan, 1981), ch. 7, 'For other than for dancing measures: *As You Like It*' (pp. 92-106).

Ideology and history

JONES-DAVIES, Marie-Thérèse, "Le monde du 'si': idéologies incertaines dans *Comme il vous plaira*," *Théâtre et idéologies: Marlowe, Shakespeare*, Actes du Congrès de la S.F.S., 1981 (Paris: Touzot, 1982), pp. 51-67.

MONTROSE, Louis Adrian, "'The Place of a Brother' in *As You Like It*: Social Process and Comic Form", *Shakespeare Quarterly*, 32 (1981), 28-54.

WILSON, Richard, "'Like the old Robin Hood': *As You Like It* and the Enclosure Riots," *Shakespeare Quarterly*, 43 (1992), 1-19. Reprinted in *Will Power: Essays on Shakespearean Authority* (Harvester Wheatsheaf, 1993), pp. 63-82.

On the structure of the play

BACHE, William B., *Design and Closure in Shakespeare's major Plays. The nature of Recapitulation.* Peter Lang, pp. 45-67.

BARTON, Anne, "*As You Like It* and *Twelfth Night*: Shakespeare's Sense of an Ending," *Shakespearean Comedy*, Stratford-upon-Avon Studies 14, ed. M. Bradbury et D. Palmer (Arnold, 1972), pp. 160-80.

On time

HALIO, Jay L., "'No clock in the forest': Time in *As You Like It*," *Studies in English Literature 1500-1900*, 2 (1962), 197-207.

TURNER, Frederick, *Shakespeare and the Nature of Time* (Oxford: Clarendon Press, 1971), pp. 28-44.

On sexuality, crossdressing, feminist approaches

BONO, Barbara J., "Mixed Gender, Mixed Genre in Shakespeare's *As You Like It*" in Barbara K. Lewalski, ed., *Renaissance Genres: Essays on Theory, History, and Interpretation* (Harvard UP, 1986), pp. 189-212.

DUSINBERRE, Juliet, "As *Who* Liked It?", *Shakespeare Survey*, 46 (1993), 9-21.

GRAS, Henk, "Enchanting Metadrama: Shakespeare and the Use of the Boy Actor in *As You Like It*," in A. J. Hoenselaars ed., *Reclamations of Shakespeare* (Rodopi, 1994), pp. 33-55.

HAYLES, Nancy K., "Sexual Disguise in *As You Like It* and

Twelfth Night," *Shakespeare Survey*, 32, 1979, 63-72.

KIMBROUGH, Robert, "Androgyny seen through Shakespeare's Disguise," *Shakespeare Quarterly*, 33, n° 1, Spring 1982, 17-33.

HOWARD, Jean E., "Crossdressing, The Theatre, and Gender Struggle in Early Modern England," *Shakespeare Quarterly*.

KOTT, Jan, "The Gender of Rosalind," *New Theatre Quarterly*, 7 (1991), 113-25.

PARK, Clara Claiborne, "As We Like It: How a Girl can be Smart and Still Popular," in C. R. S. Lenz, G. Greene et C. T. Neely eds., *The Woman's Part: Feminist Criticism of Shakespeare* (Illinois UP, 1980), pp. 100-16.

RACKIN, Phyllis, "Androgyny, Mimesis, and the Marriage of the Boy Heroine on the English Renaissance Stage," *PMLA*, vol 102, n° 1, Jan. 1987, 29-41.

SEDINGER, Tracey, "'If sight and shape be true': The Epistemology of Crossdressing on the London Stage," *Shakespeare Quarterly*, 48 (1997), 63-79.

TRAUB, Valerie, *Desire and Anxiety: Circulations of Sexuality in Shakespearean Drama* (Routledge, 1992), ch. 5, 'The Homoerotics of Shakespearean Comedy' (pp. 117-44).

WESTLUND, Joseph, *Shakespeare's Reparative Comedies* (Chicago UP, 1984), pp. 69-91.

Other approaches

GIBBONS, Brian, *Shakespeare and Multiplicity* (CUP, 1993), pp. 153-81 ('Amorous fictions in *AYL*').

GIRARD, René, *A Theater of Envy* (OUP, 1991), ch. 10, 'The Pastoral Genre in *AYL*'; 11, 'Self-Love in *AYL*' (pp. 92-105).

NEVO, Ruth, *Comic Transformations in Shakespeare* (Methuen, 1980), pp. 180-99.

WARD, John Powell, *As You Like It*, Harvester New Critical Introductions to Shakespeare (Harvester Wheatsheaf, 1992).

FENDT, Gene, "Resolution, Catharsis, Culture: *As You Like It*," *Philosophy and Literature*, 19 (1995), 248-60.

GARBER, Marjorie, "The Education of Orlando," in A. R. Braunmuller and J. C. Bulman eds, *Comedy from Shakespeare to Sheridan: Essays in Honor of Eugene M. Waith* (Associated University Presses, 1986), pp. 102-12.

GARDNER, Helen, "*As You Like It*," in *More Talking of Shakespeare*, ed. John Garrett (Longmans, 1959), pp. 17-32.

JENKINS, Harold, "*As You Like It*," *Shakespeare Survey*, 8 (1955), 40-51.

NUTTALL, A. D., "Two Unassimilable Men," *Shakespearean Comedy*, Stratford-upon-Avon Studies 14, ed. M. Bradbury et D. Palmer (Arnold, 1972), pp. 210-40.

PALMER, D. J., "Art and Nature in *As You Like It*," *Philological Quarterly*, 49 (1970), 30-40.

—, "*As You Like It* and the Idea of Play," *Critical Quarterly*, 13 (1971), 234-45.

Achevé d'imprimer le 5 février 1998
sur les presses de Dominique Guéniot,
imprimeur à Langres - Saints-Geosmes

Dépôt légal : février 1998 - N° d'imprimeur : 3175